# The
# Be…
# SE…



*Illustrated by Virginia Lister*

Beaver Books

First published in 1982 by
The Hamlyn Publishing Group Limited
London · New York · Sydney · Toronto
Astronaut House, Feltham, Middlesex, England


ISBN 0 600 20323 9

Printed and bound in Great Britain by
Cox & Wyman Limited, Reading
Set in Times

*The author and publishers gratefully acknowledge the help given to them by Elna Sewing Machines (GB) Limited, The Singer Company (UK) Limited and Style Patterns Limited in the preparation of this book.*

# *Contents*

# Basic Facts About Equipment

## *Your workbox*

A good-sized tin, about 25 cm long, 16 cm wide and 10 cm deep makes a good sewing box. So does a fruit basket with fairly deep sides. Even a small wicker shopping basket can be used, preferably a lined one.

*Suggested contents:*
a packet of assorted needles
a box of pins
a needlebook
a pincushion
scissors: cutting out; medium and embroidery
pinking shears
a tape measure
a small ruler or marking gauge
a thimble
a tracing wheel
dressmaker's carbon paper
tailor's chalk
a soft lead pencil (B or 2B)
a seam ripper
tacking thread
sewing thread
embroidery thread in a small plastic bag
paper clips, adhesive tape and glue are useful to have but they are better not mixed up with the sewing items

When sewing, have plenty of clean plastic carrier bags around. They are ideal for storing your work and keeping it perfectly clean, which is very important. If it is possible to have a special drawer for your material, this too will enable you to store it out of the dust. It is best to line the drawer.

You will need a place to work, too; preferably a good-sized table with enough space to spread your things out. Make sure that the light is adequate.

## *Tools for sewing*

**Scissors**

To hold scissors with one small and one large handle, put your thumb into the small handle and your fingers into the large one. There are many different kinds of scissors, apart from the ones described here, such as buttonhole scissors with half blades for cutting buttonhole slits, but those described below are the most useful for your workbox. Try to have one cheap pair for cutting out paper patterns or card, to avoid being tempted to use your best cutting-out and sewing scissors for these jobs, as cutting paper blunts the blades.

1 *Cutting-out scissors, also called cutting-out shears* These are large scissors with long blades for cutting through material with straight long cuts. Treasure your cutting-out scissors. Don't use them for cutting anything but material, to help keep their edges sharp and undamaged.

2 *Medium-sized scissors* Medium-sized scissors are general scissors, a size half-way between the larger cutting-out scissors and small thread-cutting or embroidery scissors. They are useful for cutting out small items and little cutting jobs, as well as for trimming seam edges. These are the most useful scissors to buy if you can only have one pair to begin with.

3 *Embroidery scissors* These are small, sharp, pointed scissors used for snipping embroidery thread, and sewing- and machine-thread ends, as well as for detailed material cutting out, such as making buttonhole slits. General thread-snipping scissors with pointed blades come in very small sizes too. In case anyone asks you what you would like for a birthday or Christmas, these make very good presents.

4 *Seam ripper* A seam ripper is a cutting tool, though

not a pair of scissors. It has a plastic handle and a sharp hook for cutting through thread. It comes in two sizes; the handier is probably the smaller size. No matter how experienced you become at sewing, there is bound to be something you will want to unpick, some mistake or change of mind to deal with. A seam ripper can be hooked under the close machine-stitch seam and will cut through the thread without damaging the material. Always put the seam ripper away in its guard cover when it is not in use.

5 *Pinking shears* These are not essential, but helpful to have. They are scissors with serrated-edged blades, which cut neat zigzags automatically, and make a pretty finish, called pinking, to the edge of material. They are especially useful for trimming the raw edges of seams for a tidy effect and to avoid fraying.

*Safety and storage* Carry scissors points down, and stick embroidery scissors' points into a cork when not in use. A large cup hook in your sewing corner can be used for hanging scissors up, one for each pair.

**Measuring tools**

Careful measuring helps you get good results from sewing, and you will find yourself using your tape measure or ruler at every stage. To begin with, for making clothes which will fit you properly, you are going to need to measure yourself. Measuring is necessary for determining the position of handles on a bag, or the place to sew buttons on a doll's dress. Here is a list of measuring tools which you could obtain. The starred ones are very important and used a lot.

1 *Tape measure** A tape measure is usually a plastic-coated tape with metal tag ends, with metric measurements (some have inches, too) along each side. The tape is about 150 cm (60 in) long, and will be marked with numbered centimetres (inches) and millimetres (fractions of an inch). In a country where metrication is new,

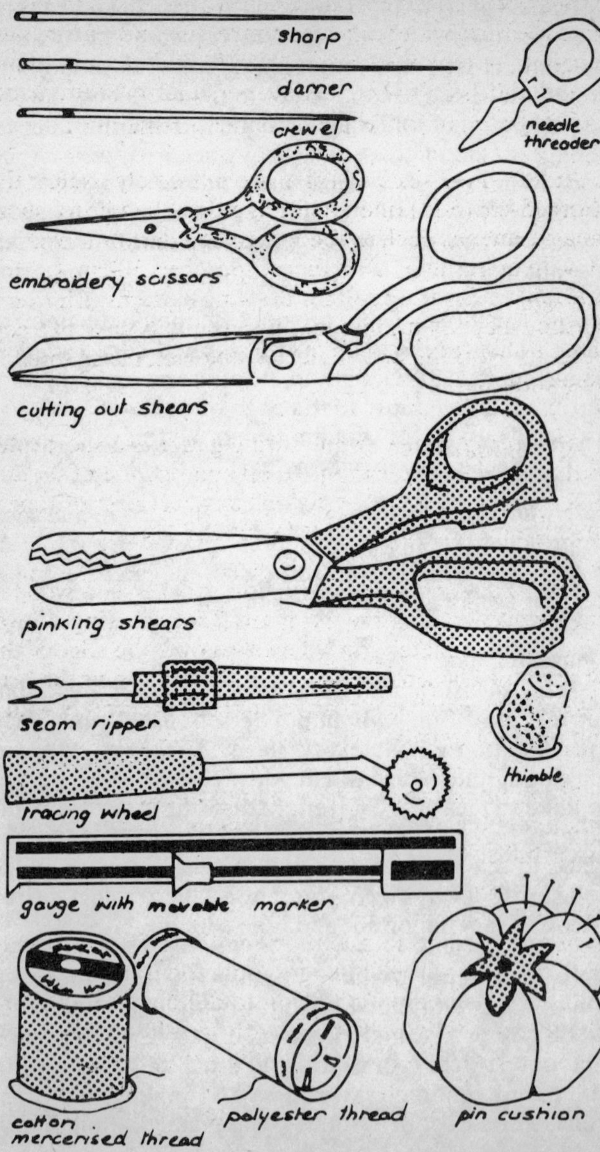
sharp
darner
crewel
needle threader
embroidery scissors
cutting out shears
pinking shears
seam ripper
thimble
tracing wheel
gauge with movable marker
cotton mercerised thread
polyester thread
pin cushion

or has not yet been introduced, it is a good idea to have a tape measure with both centimetres and inches for comparison. A tape measure is flexible and can be wound round the body when taking personal measurements (see page 63) or for long length measurements.

2 *Ruler** Two sizes of ruler are extremely useful: the short 15-cm (6-in) ruler, which is easy to handle for short measurements, such as the length of a dart or the depth of a hem turning, and the all-purpose 30-cm (12-in) ruler, for measuring and for drawing patterns. Choose a plastic ruler for preference, because it is easy to keep clean for working with material, and won't snag threads by splintering.

3 *Measuring gauge* A measuring gauge is a short ruler with a marker you can move up and down and set at a given point. It is handy for instant checking of repeat measurements such as a hem depth all along.

4 *Hem marker* The hem or skirt marker is a wooden ruler which stands on the floor for measuring a level hem. It has a metal arm which clips over the edge of the skirt at the chosen distance from the floor, plus the hem allowance, which can then be marked accurately with a pin or tailor's chalk.

5 *Metre or yardstick* This is a long wooden ruler useful when making items with large lengths of material, such as curtains.

**Marking tools**

When you come to making something from a bought pattern, you will need some tools for transferring the pattern construction marks on to the material. Tailor's chalk and pins are very frequently used for quick marking in sewing.

1 *Tailor's chalk* This is smooth-textured hard chalk

which you can use to draw on material, and which brushes away later. It is whitish-grey, or pinkish-beige in colour.

2 *Tracing wheel* This is a metal or plastic wheel with serrated edges, fitted into a handle like the front wheel of a wheelbarrow. Combined with dressmaker's carbon paper, and with the help of a ruler, it is rolled over material with the pattern pinned on, to print the pattern marks in the form of carbon dots on the fabric.

3 *Dressmaker's carbon paper* These are small sheets of special carbon paper for use in sewing. The packet usually contains different coloured sheets to show up on different colours of material.

**Needles**

Stone-age people who lived in caves used to use needles made of fishbone, animal bone or ivory. They were as large as bodkins, but then they were used for lacing skins together with leather thongs. When ways of making metal were discovered, needles were then made of it, fashioned, ground and polished by hand.

We are luckier. We have the advantage of strong, highly polished, rustless steel needles and pins, and a wide choice of different types each with its own special purpose: needles for sewing hats, called milliner's or straws; beading needles for threading beads; wedge-tipped needles for sewing leather, and many other kinds. For your sewing box, the best to buy for your requirements at first would be a packet of assorted needles, sometimes called a household pack. Here are the main ones you'd use.

1 *Sharps* Sharps are the basic needles in the pack for all sorts of sewing jobs. They are a plain shape with an oval hole, or 'eye' for passing the thread through. Useful sizes are 6, 7 and the larger 9, for sewing thicker, stiffer material. Sharps are used for hemming, oversewing, backstitch and other stitches used for hand sewing.

2 *Darners* Darners are longer, slimmer needles than sharps. They have a long egg-shaped eye for use with embroidery thread or fine wool darning yarn. A small darner with ordinary thread is good for tacking. Double long or wool darners are available for thicker wool.

3 *Crewel* Crewel is the name given to embroidery needles. They are short and have a large eye to enable the embroidery thread to pass through easily. If you haven't got a crewel needle a small darner is a good substitute.

There is another kind of embroidery needle called a tapestry needle. This is stumpier than a crewel needle and has a larger eye, because it is usually threaded with thicker embroidery yarn, or tapestry wool. It has a blunt tip and is usually used for embroidery on canvas to push through the holes easily. A sharp pointed needle would catch in the canvas.

**Needle threader**

In case you ever need to use a needle threader, this is a thin metal disc with a fine wire loop sticking out from the side. To use it, press the sides of the wire loop together and push it through the eye of the needle. When it reaches the other side the loop will spring open. Pass the thread through the loop and draw it back through the eye, then take the thread end out of the loop.

**Pins**

Pins are used for fastening material shapes together to hold them in place before tacking and stitching, and for pinning paper patterns on the material. They are useful also as markers and guidelines. Use rustless steel pins (and throw a rusty pin away if ever you find one). The pretty pins with plastic knobs on the top are easy to use, but a little more expensive to buy. Store needles in a needlebook or back in their packet, and pins in their box or pincushion. Always put needles away after use. A needle lost in the carpet or upholstery can hurt or give a worse injury if it sticks into someone accidentally, and can severely injure a dog or cat if it gets into a paw.

**Magnet**

A small magnet will pick up fallen pins more quickly than the most nimble fingers, so it is a good idea to keep one in your workbox.

**Thimble**

A thimble is a cap for the middle finger of your sewing hand, made of silver, metal or plastic. There is sure to be one to fit your size. Choose one that is a close, comfortable fit. The little dents over it are to press on the needle end when pushing it through material. Without a thimble, repeated stitches will soon make your finger sore, and to hold the needle between your finger and thumb lessens the pressure of pushing. You will definitely need a thimble for sewing extra thick or stiff material.

## *Thread*

When choosing thread, look at the label to see what kind of fibre it is made of, such as cotton, or polyester, and how thick it is. The number on it will tell you: 50 is thin thread; 40 is medium thread and 30 is thicker and used for machine embroidery.

Try to match your material not only for colour, but for fibre too. The following table will help you to decide which thread you need for the sewing job in hand.

| | |
|---|---|
| **tacking (or basting) thread** | *cheap black or white thread for tacking, which is taken out after sewing has been completed and thrown away* |
| **cotton thread** | *matt cotton thread used for making cotton sheets, or clothes made of strong cotton material* |

| | |
|---|---|
| **mercerised cotton thread** | *silky-looking cotton thread, usually number 40, but also numbers 50 and 30, used for sewing cotton or wool material and fabrics made from natural fibres* |
| **polyester or Terylene thread** | *thread made of synthetic fibres suitable for sewing synthetic materials* |
| **poly-cotton** | *a mixture of polyester and cotton made into 4-ply sewing thread* |
| **silk thread** | *silk thread, sold on tiny cardboard spools, used for tacking and sewing luxury materials such as pure silk and velvet* |
| **elastic thread** | *elastic thread is used for elastic shirring (see page 103)* |
| **button thread** | *extra strong cotton thread for tough sewing jobs, such as sewing on coat buttons* |
| **embroidery thread: stranded embroidery cotton** | *choose one which says* fast colour. *Six-stranded cotton which comes in skeins. To use, draw the end of the thread out from the skein, carefully, and cut a length of about 30 cm. Separate the strands to the number you wish to use* |
| **soft embroidery cotton** | *this is like soft thin coloured string. It is especially good for embroidering felt or canvas, with cross stitch and other stitches* |
| **tapisserie wool** | *fine wool, sold in skeins, used for tapestry work and for embroidering wool or felt* |

An embroidery ring is a double wooden ring in which you can clamp your embroidery to make the material taut as a drum-skin, and therefore easy to stitch evenly.

**To match the thread**

You will need to suit the colour of the thread to your material. Take a scrap of fabric with you, and choose matching or slightly darker thread to go with it. If you have flowered or patterned material with lots of different colours, select the thread colour to match the background.

## *Material*

When you go shopping for material, choose carefully. Apart from its looks, or whether it is for summer or winter, or would make whatever you have in mind, a material's particular features can make a lot of difference to your success with the finished item and are worth knowing about.

**Woven or knitted?**

*Woven material* is made of long threads stretched on a loom (warp threads) and threads woven in and out across them (weft or woof threads). The way the cross-threads are woven in and out, one for one, or in steps, or jumping several warp threads at a time, gives the material a particular surface. And, of course, different coloured threads are often used too.

*Knitted material* is made up of knitted threads like a pullover. Some knitted material is firm and some is soft and stretchy. It can be made in cotton or polyester for summer, or wool or acrylic for winter. It may stretch one way only, from side to side, or up and down as well, called two-way stretch. Knitted material is comfortable to wear, but is sometimes a little more difficult to sew than woven material because of its stretchiness.

*Non-woven material* Felt is non-woven; so is some interfacing fabric, that is, the stiffening placed between layers of material and the lining of collars and cuffs, to prevent them being droopy. Non-woven material is made by compressing fibres together.

**Synthetic or natural fibres?**
Synthetic fibres are made industrially out of coal and oil by-products. Nylon is synthetic; so is polyester. These fibres are usually strong and won't shrink. Materials made from them need a similar fibre lining, and to be stitched with synthetic thread, too, so that all the parts are alike for durability, cleaning and washing, so one part does not shrink more than another.

Natural fibres have been familiar for thousands of years: sheep's wool, silk, cotton, linen. They are beautiful and comfortable but are liable to shrink and crease unless specially treated. They too should be lined with similar fibres to themselves, although manufactured rayon goes well with them as lining. And they should be sewn with cotton, silk or linen thread suited to their texture and thickness. You can get mixed natural and synthetic fibres too. These are all factors to bear in mind when you are shopping.

**Shopping for material**
Material is stacked usually in rolls or bales, or hanging from racks for velvet or fur fabric. Look at the label. It will tell you the price per metre (or yard); the fibre or blended fibres it is made of; usually if it is washable (don't buy it if it isn't, or it could cost a fortune in dry cleaning bills eventually) and the width of the material.

If the material is very wide, you won't require as long an amount as you would if it were narrower. A bought pattern will give you the right amount to buy for all the different material widths (see page 146).

*material widths*

| | |
|---|---|
| 90 cm | 36 in |
| 115 cm | 45 in |
| 140 cm | 54 in |
| 160 cm | 60 in |

*other features to check*
Is it washable . . . or do you have to pay for it to be dry cleaned? Crease-resisting, or does it crumple in your hand if you squeeze it? Drip-dry, or will it need pressing when washed? Dye-fast or does the dye run out when it is washed (into other washing!)? Flame retardant? This is important for nightclothes or net party dresses.

**Material facts**
Look at a piece of your material. There are some things to know about it which will help you when you come to cutting out and sewing. Decide first whether it is woven or knitted and read on.

*Woven material* The woven edges along the sides of the material are called *selvages* (or selvedges). The edge across the cut ends of the material is called the *raw edge*. Up and down the length of the material, parallel with the selvages, is called the *lengthwise grain* or the *straight grain of fabric*. Across the material from selvage to selvage is called the *crosswise grain*. The diagonal of the material is called the *bias*. When you cut material on the bias, you will discover it is rather stretchy.

*Knitted material* Knitted material is usually soft and stretchy and can be rather tricky to sew. Use lots of pins to keep it in shape when pinning on the pattern for cutting out. Use ballpoint needles if you can get hold of them, or a new sharp needle. When cutting out allow wider seam allowances as knitted material has a tendency to curl at the edges. Instead of placing the pattern 'straight grain of fabric' symbol on the lengthwise grain (see page 151) follow the direction of knit up and down the material. Sew tape in with the armhole or waist seams to stop the stretchiness flopping.

*Right side and wrong side* Material has a 'right side' and a 'wrong side' unless it is reversible like check gingham, when it is the same on both sides. With printed material, the best and brightest pattern and colours are the 'right side', as is the best side of woven material, where the smartest surface shows. The duller, rougher side with more faint or faded colouring is the 'wrong side'.

*Right sides (and wrong sides) facing* In sewing you constantly come across the terms: 'right sides facing' or 'wrong sides facing', as well as 'right sides out' or 'wrong sides out'. And sometimes the wrong side can face the right side!

*Facing* means placed together; *out* means showing on the outside; so *right sides facing* means that the right sides are together like the inside of a sandwich, and the same goes for *wrong sides facing*, when it's the turn of the wrong sides to be the inside of the sandwich.

*Right sides out* means the right sides are showing on the outside, and *wrong sides out* means that the wrong sides should be showing on the outside.

*Wrong side facing right side* (or vice versa): this happens sometimes, such as when an edge is being faced on to the right side. (See page 143.)

*With nap* When material is said to be 'with nap' it means that it has a surface which goes one way, like the fur on a cat's back. Velvet is with nap, so are corduroy, needlecord and some fur fabrics. Material with nap always has to be sewn with the different parts cut out in the same direction, or when it is made up the surface will catch the light unequally, and one part will give the impression of being lighter than the other. You can feel by stroking with nap material the way the furry surface lies. (See page 153 for a 'with nap' layout.)

*Plaids, stripes, one-way and bold patterns* When joining plaid or striped material together, make sure that the bands of colour or design match at the seams or the effect will look disjointed.

Allow extra material when you are shopping to take account of repeat check patterns of fancy designs in the fabric, to give you room to shift the pattern on it when you are cutting out.

*Straight and true* The printed pattern or plaid bands on your material should be in line with the selvage, and the selvages of the material should be straight too, not with one longer than the other, giving it a wavy edge. If your material is like this pull it to and fro to straighten it. Cut along a crosswise thread to make sure the ends are straight too, before cutting out.

*Pre-shrunk* Cotton fabric such as denim or cheesecloth can be pre-shrunk by washing in clear water, then drying and pressing, before cutting out. Woollen material can be pre-shrunk by pressing it under a very damp press cloth first.

*Material economy* You can often buy short lengths of material, the ends of rolls and other oddments, which are plenty long enough to make something for yourself, and often much cheaper than buying material off a roll. These ends are called remnants. Look for the remnants counter or at the end of the sales counter in the shop for them.

Material often comes folded in half from selvage to selvage. When cutting out, refold it to accommodate the pattern so you save as much as you can for making other things.

**Glossary of materials**

*Acrylic* Synthetic, bulky material. Often used for knitted fabrics.

*Brushed rayon* Brushed woven material like heavy cotton. Easy to sew.

*Calico* Coarse woven cotton, usually a natural cream colour.

*Cheesecloth* Filmy, crêpe cotton. It needs pre-shrinking before sewing.

*Corduroy* Ribbed velvety material, usually made of cotton.

*Cotton jersey* T-shirt material. Sew following the rules for knits.

*Cotton sateen* Furnishing material used for curtain lining. Good for stage costumes.

*Denim* Coarse blue cotton jeans material. Available in other colours.

*Felt* Matted material in bright colours. Easy to sew but not washable.

*Flannel* Smooth woven wool material (or other fibres) used for school blazers.

*Fur fabric* Often made of synthetic fibres. Use with a 'with nap' cutting layout. (See page 153.)

*Gingham* Woven check cotton material. Reversible, that is, without a right and wrong side.

*Hessian* Sacking. Cheap and available in a wide range of good colours.

*Jersey* Knitted fabric, made in wool, cotton or synthetic fibres.

*Lawn* Fine woven cotton material; not expensive.

*Linen* Woven material made from the flax plant. Good imitations are available.

*Needlecord* Very fine ribbed corduroy. Easy to sew.

*Nylon* Tough woven or knitted synthetic material, with a silky look.

*Polyester* Synthetic material made up in many different ways: knitted or woven. Practical and popular.

*Poplin* Woven cotton with a slight silky sheen.

*Quilting* Padded stitched material which is available in

cotton, nylon and a number of other fabrics.
*Rayon* Artificial silk, the oldest type of man-made material. Also made like heavy woven cotton and in other versions.
*Satin* Shiny surfaced party dress material.
*Silk* Luxurious fine material spun by silkworms.
*Stretch terry* Stretchy knitted towelling.
*Taffeta* Stiff papery silky material, the cheap kind used for lining.
*Tartan* Scottish plaid fabric.
*Terylene* Woven or knitted synthetic material.
*Towelling* Cotton fabric with a looped surface, sometimes on both sides.
*Tweed* Type of woven wool: e.g. Harris tweed is strong, rough and thick; Irish Donegal tweed is prettily speckled. There are also tweed-look synthetic materials.
*Velvet* Plush-surface material. Sew with a 'with nap' cutting layout. (See page 153.)
*Velveteen* A cheaper form of cotton velvet.
*Vilene* Useful non-woven interfacing suited to most home sewing.
*Winceyette* Woven cotton flannelette pyjama material.
*Wool* Made from the sheep's fleece, and can be knitted or woven; fine or thick. Usually dry cleaned.

'Notions' are all the odds and ends used to make things in sewing. Here is a glossary explaining what they all are.

**Glossary of notions**
*Beads* For embroidery or necklaces.
*Belting* Stiff belt interfacing.
*Bias binding* Bought bias edging strip.
*Braid* Fancy or plain strip for trimming or edging, or used instead of tape.
*Broderie anglaise* Eyelet-hole embroidered material, also used for trimming.
*Buckles* Belt or strap fastenings measured across the centre bar.

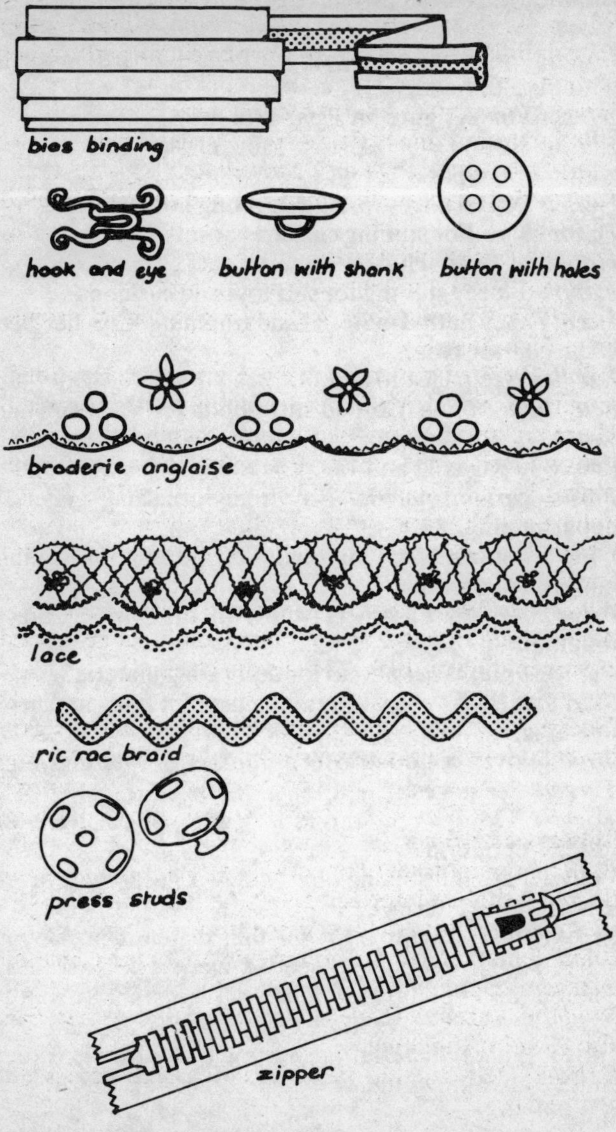
bias binding
hook and eye
button with shank
button with holes
broderie anglaise
lace
ric rac braid
press studs
zipper

*Buttons* Measured by diameter: may be with holes or a shank.
*Cutting board* Cutting-out cardboard board marked with measurements.
*Dress form* A figure on a stand for fitting garments.
*Elastic* Round hat elastic; baby elastic and various widths and types.
*Eyelets* Metal edges for buckle prong holes in belts.
*Foam chips* For stuffing cushions or soft toys.
*Hooks and eyes* Hook fasteners.
*Kapok* Fleecy stuffing for soft toys and cushions.
*Lace* Fancy netted material and trimming. Crochet lace is the coarser type.
*Needles* See pages 10 and 11.
*Petersham ribbon* Corded stiff ribbon for waist and hat bands.
*Pins* See pages 11 and 12.
*Plastic curtain material* Buy from furnishing material department.
*PVC* Plastic-coated material; buy from furnishing material department.
*Press fasteners* Fasteners with two sides which press together.
*Ric-rac braid* Wavy braid for decorating material.
*Skirt tape* Narrow woven ribbon tape for seam and hem finishing.
*Tape* Woven cotton strip for apron ties, drawstrings, etc.
*Thread* See pages 12 and 13.
*Toggles* Horn, wood or plastic pegs fastened by a loop instead of buttons.
*Velcro* Patent fastening tape with two sides which press together and interlock.
*Zip fasteners* Lightweight for thin material; metal for skirts and trousers; open-ended zippers for anoraks. There are lots of different kinds.

Note: Where material is illustrated in this book the shaded area shows the *wrong side*; the white area shows the *right side*.

# Hand Sewing

Before sewing machines were invented, everyone's clothes had to be made by hand. So not owning a sewing machine needn't prevent you from sewing. Even if you have one, there is always quite a lot of hand sewing to be done to any item.

Here are some of the main stitches that crop up often; there are hundreds of others, especially in embroidery, but the ones described here should be enough to go on with. Before you start you will need to thread the needle and make a knot in the thread end.

**To thread a needle**

1 Cut about 30 cm of sewing thread.

2 Snip the thread end with a fresh clean cut to stop any wisps of thread sticking out.

3 Dampen the trimmed thread between your lips and point it towards the eye of the needle.

4 Pass the dampened thread end through the eye of the needle for about 6 to 7 cm.

**To make a knot in the thread end**

1 Hold the threaded needle level. Take the tail end of the thread and wind it twice round the point of the needle.

2 Hold this wound thread tightly in place with one hand, while you take hold of the needle point with the other hand and draw it through the knot with all the thread length after it. Do this smoothly and a knot will form.

**To thread wool**

1 Choose a large darner or wool needle. Double the wool over the needle point and pinch it on to it with your finger and thumb.

2 Draw the wool off the needle still pinched together. Push the pinched together wool, still folded, through the eye of the needle and draw it through to the other side.

## *Hand stitches*

(Knot the thread end each time unless otherwise specified.)

**Tacking**

This means long, level stitches for securing sewing before stitching properly. It is also used for tacking guidelines to mark material. Use tacking or sewing thread, with a fairly long length of thread, about 35 cm, and a small darner needle. Start from the right-hand side of the material.

1 Put the needle into the material level and bring it out 1 cm–2 cm further along level.

2 Draw the thread through.

3 Put the needle in again level about 1.5 cm–2.5 cm further along and bring it out again 1 cm–2 cm later. Continue for the row.

4 Finish with a long, loose backstitch and snip the thread, leaving a fairly long tail.

To remove tacking, pull the end backstitch out by putting a needle under it to draw it out, then pull the knot and draw the thread back out of the material.

**Running stitch**

This has short level stitches with equal spaces between. It is used for simple seams and for securing braid and other light hand-sewing jobs. A second row of running stitch in the spaces left by the first using a different colour is called *double running stitch*, and is used for decoration.

1 Bring the needle through from the wrong side of the material at the beginning of the stitch line on the right.

2 Draw the thread right through.

3 Put the needle in and out level for two stitches and spaces, in the same way as tacking but with stitches and spaces of equal length.

4 Continue for the row. Finish off with two or three small backstitches on the wrong side.

**Hemming stitch**

This is used for securing hems or sewing on appliqué shapes. Push the needle under the folded edge of the tacked hem working from the wrong side of the material, and starting at the right. Bring the needle through the hem close above the fold.

2 Draw the thread through.

3 Pass the needle through the material just below the hem at a slight diagonal, a stitch to the left and pick up two or three threads. Pull the thread through. Repeat for the row, taking care to keep the stitches evenly sized and not to draw them too tight, so the hem puckers. To finish, oversew the hem fold twice and take the needle through the hem fold and out. Snip the thread close to the material.

**Slipstitch**

This is similar to hemming, but the long stitch is made into the turning of the hem so that the stitching is invisible on the right side of the material. Bring the needle through the fold of the turning, starting from the right, and pick up a thread in the material. Slip the needle back through the first fold for a stitch then come across and pick up another thread. Secure the thread at the end with two or three oversewing stitches.

**Backstitch**

Backstitch is a row of close, level stitches which look like machine straight stitching on the right side. It is used for strong seams or decoration. Several backstitches made on the same spot are used for securing thread or stitches when starting or finishing.

1 Backstitch starts on the right. Bring the needle through for the beginning of the row from the wrong side, or from between the layers if you are sewing a seam.

2 Take a level stitch back and put the needle in. Bring it out a stitch's length ahead and level with the previous stitch and draw the thread through.

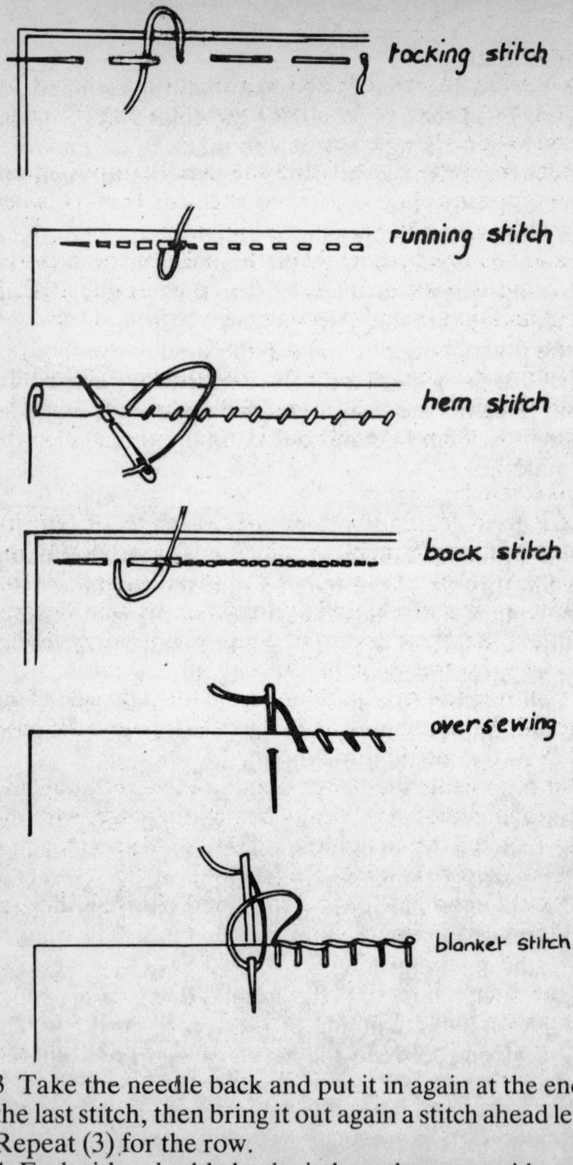


3 Take the needle back and put it in again at the end of the last stitch, then bring it out again a stitch ahead level. Repeat (3) for the row.
4 End with a double backstitch on the wrong side.

**Oversewing**

For finishing a raw edge of felt or on a seam, or for joining two pieces of material together along the edge, oversewing is the stitch used.

1 Start from the right. Bring the needle through from the wrong side close below the edge (or from between the two layers if they are being joined).

2 Take the needle back over the edge of the material and bring it back through to the front again, a stitch along and just below the edge as before. Draw the thread through.

3 Continue oversewing for the row and finish off with a double oversewing stitch. Take the thread between the layers or to the wrong side, and trim.

**Blanket stitch**

This is used for finishing an edge, such as of felt; for securing a single hem on thick material, when the blanket stitches are the depth of the turning; for embroidering round a simple buttonhole; and for decoration. Use the appropriate thread – embroidery thread or wool – for the job in hand.

1 Start from the right, working from the right side of the material. Bring the needle through just below the edge and draw the thread through.

2 Put the needle in a stitch length below the edge and point the needle up vertically behind the edge, with the thread looped round the back of the needle point.

3 Draw the thread right through.

Repeat (2) and (3) for the row, and oversew the last stitch twice to secure.

**Chain stitch**

This is used mainly for embroidery.

1 Start at the beginning of the row, and bring the thread through from the wrong side for the beginning of the first stitch. Chain stitch usually begins somewhere on the right side of the material, where your planned embroidery design starts. Hold the material so that the first

stitch will be positioned at the top of the row.
2 Put the needle back into the material beside where the thread came out and bring the needle out a stitch length below with the thread behind the needle point. Draw the thread through, leaving a small loop.
3 Put the needle in again, this time inside the chain loop, and beside where the thread came out and bring the needle out again a stitch below, with the thread behind the needle point. Repeat for the row, ending with a double oversewing stitch over the last loop, then two or three small backstitches on the wrong side.

**Lazy-daisy**
A lazy-daisy is a wheel of chain stitch petals. Bring the needle through at the centre of the daisy, and make a chain stitch. Take the thread across the lower end of the stitch and put the needle in, then bring it out again at the centre of the flower once more. Repeat for the wheel of stitches and end with two or three backstitches on the wrong side.

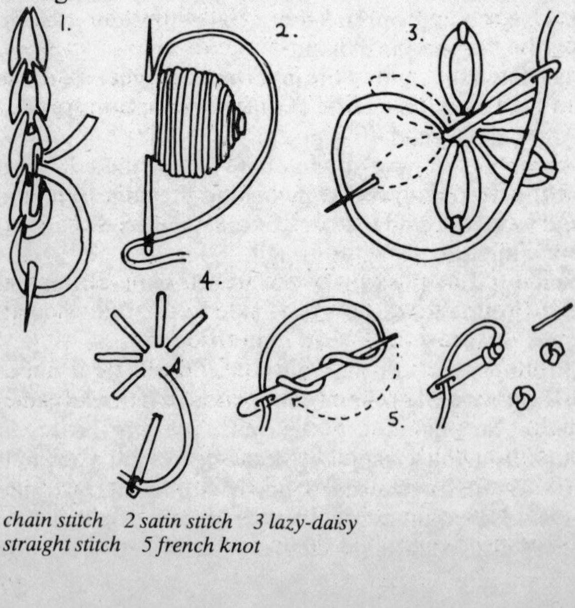


*1 chain stitch 2 satin stitch 3 lazy-daisy*
*4 straight stitch 5 french knot*

**Straight stitch**

A simple stitch for wool and other embroidery, such as for sewing doll's eyelashes.

1 Bring the thread through from the wrong side to the right side for the beginning of the first stitch. Draw the thread right through.

2 Put the needle in again at the other end of the stitch and bring it out again for the start of the next stitch.

**Satin stitch**

Satin stitch is used for embroidery, for filling in shapes such as leaves or a doll's mouth, and it features in practical sewing too, such as making bar ends to button-holes. For embroidery, draw the shape to be filled in with a pencil or outline it with tiny running stitches.

1 Bring the needle through from the wrong side for the beginning of the first stitch on the left-hand outline of the design, at one end.

2 Put the needle in at the opposite side of the design on the outline, either horizontally or diagonally.

3 Bring the needle out again on the outline exactly beside the beginning of the first stitch and put it in again exactly beside the end of the first stitch. Repeat until the whole shape has been filled in with smooth satin stitch.

**French knot**

A decorative raised dot for embroidery, made with embroidery thread. Mark its position with tailor's chalk or pencil.

1 Decide on the position of the french knot. Bring the needle through from the wrong side to the right side at this spot and draw the thread right through.

2 Put the needle into the material, and bring it out a small distance along, close beside where the thread came through.

3 Press the needle against the material with your left hand while you wind the thread, the lower part near the material, round the point twice with your right hand. Keep the needle pressed down and carefully draw the

needle and thread right through the knot so that it remains on the surface of the material.
4 Put the needle into the material again close by the knot to secure it. Take the needle along under the material on the wrong side, and bring it through again at the position of the next french knot, or secure the thread on the wrong side with two or three backstitches.

**Starting and finishing hand sewing**
A knot in the end of the thread will prevent the thread from slipping out of the material when you begin to sew, but for loosely woven fabric such as wool the thread may need to be secured with two or three backstitches sewn on the same spot, not in a line, as well as a knot. To finish, two or three backstitches sewn on top of one another on the wrong side of the material, if possible so they hardly show on the right side, will secure a stitch-line. Two or three oversewing stitches on the same spot are more suitable for finishing hem or edge stitches. Where possible, draw the thread through between layers of material and trim it close to the surface, to conceal the end.

**To hold hand sewing**
Place the part of the material you are sewing over your forefinger of your left hand (if right-handed, or vice versa, if left-handed) and pinch it together with your thumb and middle finger. Stitch along this part, then when complete, move over to the next part in the same way. An embroidery ring helps when sewing embroidery stitches.

**Plain seam**
A plain seam joins two shapes together. There are other types of seam, but this is the basic one most generally used. It consists of the *stitchline*, the row of stitches used to make the seam; the *seam allowance*, the distance between the stitchline and the edge of the material; and the *raw edge*, that is, the cut edge. To make a plain seam

follow the steps which are described below:
1 With right sides facing, match the raw edges of the material and the notches (the triangular points which stick out from the side of the material) if you used a bought paper pattern when cutting out. Pin along the seam allowance close to the stitchline to secure the pieces together.
2 Tack the seam close above or below the stitchline and remove the pins as you go.
3 For hand sewing the seam use backstitch or running stitch, or adjust your sewing machine to straight stitches the right length, for your material. For knitted material seams, see pages 110 and 111.

If sewing by hand, proceed from the beginning of the seam and continue to the end.

For a machine-stitched seam, place the beginning of the stitchline under the machine needle two or three stitches in. Reverse for a few stitches then machine along the seam. Reverse for two or three stitches at the end (not for zigzag or machine stitch patterns).
4 Remove the tacking thread.
5 Open the material and the seam allowances out. Press the seam open with an iron.
6 Finish the raw edges of the seam allowance choosing the most suitable method for your material.

*To finish seams* you can do one of the following:
1 Trim the raw edge close to the edge with pinking shears.
2 Oversew the seam raw edges by hand.
3 Zigzag machine stitch finish: adjust the sewing machine to large zigzag stitch. Fold back the material so the seam allowance is to one side, and place the edge of the seam allowance under the machine needle. Zigzag stitch all along by the edge and repeat for the other side.
4 Turn a narrow hem along the edge of the seam allowance on to the seam allowance wrong side, and machine with straight stitches. (On very thick material, seams are sometimes finished by edging with bias binding.)

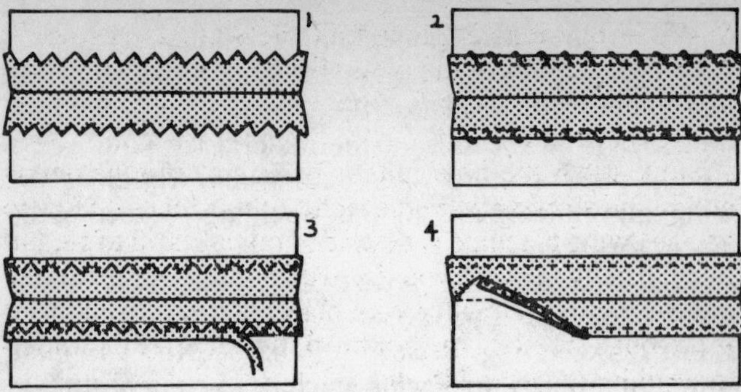


*Seam finishes: 1 pinked 2 oversewn 3 zigzag stitched 4 hemmed*

**Plain hem**

A plain hem is the straight hem that you might turn along the edges of a handkerchief or sheet. Skirts and dresses usually have shaped hems, and although they are similar in many ways to a plain hem there is a little more to making them. It helps to first know how to turn a basic hem. You will need a ruler, measuring gauge or tape measure, as well as pins, a needle, tacking thread, sewing thread, and equipment for pressing the finished hem.
1 Place the item being hemmed on the table wrong side up, with the edge to be hemmed at the top facing you.
2 Turn over the raw edge on to the wrong side, to a depth of about 1 cm, or less for a narrow hem.
3 Turn over this folded edge again to the required hem depth. This is measured in the following way. Suppose it is 5 cm. Place the ruler against the hem with the end against the folded edge and measure 5 cm along the ruler. Mark the material with a pin at this point, then turn over the edge so this mark is along the fold. Remove the marker pin and pin the hem in place.
4 Continue to turn and pin the hem to this depth, checking the depth of the turning as you go. This is where a gauge with a movable marker comes in useful. Set the gauge to the measurement for your hem, and place it across the hem all along to make sure you have turned over the right amount.

5 When the hem is pinned all the way along, tack it about 0.75 cm from the pinned edge, removing the pins as you proceed.

6 Press the hem.

7 Now stitch the hem, either by hand using hemming stitch and starting from the right; or machine it. How to use a sewing machine is described on pages 50 to 58, but here, briefly, is what you do. Adjust the machine to the stitch length suitable for your material thickness and put matching thread on the bobbin and needle. (For knitted materials see pages 110 and 111.)

Place the tacked hem edge under the needle, with the wrong side of the material uppermost. Reverse for a few stitches at the beginning, then machine along the hem close to the edge, using the inside of the presser foot as a guide for a straight stitch line. Reverse for a few stitches at the end.

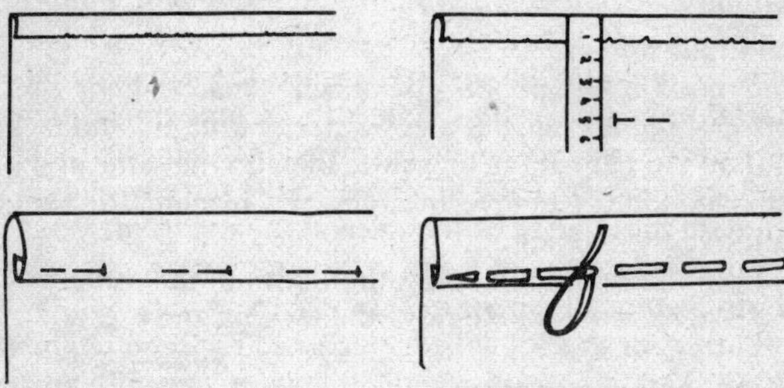

**Hem corner**

Prepare the hem corner while you are turning and pinning the hem.

1 Trim off the corner to within 0.75 cm of the finished hems. Turn under this trimmed edge 0.75 cm and fold the hem corner over diagonally. Repeat for the other sides. Pin down and tack the corner, then oversew or slipstitch the join. See pages 38 and 39 for another way to mitre a corner.

2 When machining the hem, stop at the corner with the needle in the material, raise the presser foot and pivot

the material round the corner on the needle. Lower the presser foot and continue machining along the other side.

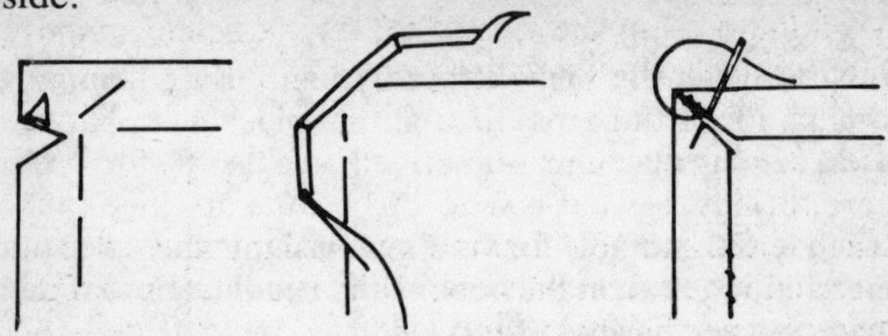

*Hem corner on thin material* If you turn a narrow 0.50-cm hem along the edges of a silk or lawn scarf, or some other item, there won't be room to mitre the corner. Finish the hem completely along the sides, then turn over the hem along the other side to form an L-shape at the corner.

**Hemming a scarf**

You need a square of silk or silky material, or thin cotton: 50 cm square is a good size. Turn, pin and tack an 0.50-cm hem along one side, then do the same at the opposite side. Remove the pins and machine or hem. Remove the tacking.

Turn the hem along the other sides in the same way and stitch them too. Remove the tacking and press.

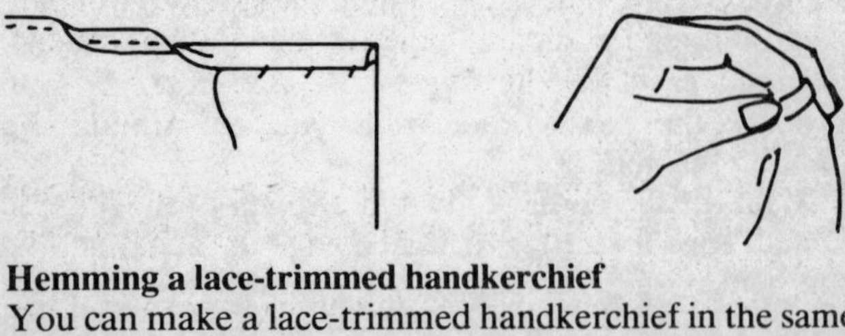

**Hemming a lace-trimmed handkerchief**

You can make a lace-trimmed handkerchief in the same way, with a 25-cm to 30-cm square of lawn, cotton or silk, and lace trimming to equal the length of the four sides plus enough to overlap the ends. Hem the square as for the scarf. Pin the lace woven edge right side facing against the hem on the wrong side of the handkerchief, pleating the lace at the corners, tack it and remove the pins. Overlap the ends as for tape (see page 48). Machine or hem the lace to the handkerchief, remove the tacking and press with an iron.

## *Bias binding*

Bias binding is the method of finishing the edge of material with a neat band of fabric. Bias means that the strip of material from which the binding is made is cut out diagonally from woven material so it has a stretchy quality and fits over the edge better. Knitted material doesn't work for this purpose because it doesn't have a bias and is usually too bulky.

If you wish to bind an edge, you will need either to cut out some bias strips of material yourself, or to buy some special bias binding already made. This is usually made of fine cotton and is sold in various widths, starting with the familiar 12-mm (½-in) binding. It usually comes on cards with several metres of binding.

Cutting your own bias strip can save you money, and it means you can use material (provided it is not too thick) to match or contrast with the main fabric. Cotton material with flowers or stripes makes smart bias binding, and satin is suitable too, and very pretty.

Buying ready-made bias binding will save you trouble, because it comes already joined in a long strip with the edges turned in to help you.

**To cut a bias strip**

To cut out your own bias strip you will need a square of material at least 30 cm in size, a ruler, pins, tailor's chalk or a pencil and scissors.

1 Draw a line diagonally from corner to corner of the square of material, or use pins as markers.

2 Mark other rows an equal distance from the first, enough for the length you are going to need eventually when the strips are joined together: 4 cm is a good width.

3 Cut out the strips you need along the marked lines.
4 To join the strips, place two together right sides facing at right angles to one another. Pin and tack them across where shown, then backstitch or machine with straight stitches where tacked.
5 Add other pieces to the strip until you have the length you require.
6 Remove the tacking and press the seams open, then press the entire strip from the right side. Trim the edges level all along. Bias strip like this is used for facing as well as binding.

**To sew on bias binding**

The procedure is the same for home-made or bought bias binding.
1 Place the raw edge of the bias binding right sides facing against the raw edge of the material. For bought bias binding open out one folded edge to do this.
2 Pin the binding to the material just above the crease for bought tape or 1 cm from the edge for home-made 4-cm wide bias binding. Tack where pinned, removing the pins as you go.
3 Leave about 1 cm unstitched at the beginning and end for turning in or overlapping when finishing off. Sew the binding to the material by hand with backstitch, or by machine with straight stitch, in the crease for bought bias binding, close by the tacking for home-made.
4 Turn the wrong side towards you. To turn the binding to the wrong side, the fold of bought bias binding is pinned on, but you will need to turn under the edge of home-made binding 1 cm before pinning it in place.

Pull the turned under binding over the edge to the wrong side a few centimetres at a time, stretching it slightly for a neat fit, and pin it in place just above the stitchline which shows through from the front of the material. Tack where pinned and remove the pins.
5 Starting from the right, hem the binding to the wrong side where tacked, avoiding any stitches showing through on the right side.

*Ends* Turn in the binding at each end and hem, or overlap one turned-in end over the other, and hem in place.

*Corners* Fold the binding so that the fold is parallel with the edge and forms a diagonal pleat across the corner. Pin. Stitch by hand with backstitch, just half-way across and remove the pin. When the first part is complete, and the binding is turned to the wrong side, make a pleat at the corner and hem or oversew the pleat in place by hand.

**Facing**
Facing with bias binding or bias strip is useful for finishing an edge where there isn't enough material to spare to turn a hem, or to finish an edge where the material is too thick to turn. Facing can be used for lengthening a hem too, so the old hem can be added to the length of the garment.

Facing made of pretty material such as satin can be made on the right side for decoration. On the wrong side bought wide bias binding or taffeta lining bias strip are the best materials to use.

Shaped facings are another way of facing. They are cut out to match the garment shape.

**Facing for a hem**
1 Place the facing strip right sides facing so the facing edge and the material edge match. Pin and tack as for bias binding (2). At the end, allow 1.5 cm extra for a seam across the facing, or to turn in at each end to

neaten. Remove the pins and backstitch or machine. Remove the tacking. Seam the facing across at this stage, if required.

2 Turn the facing over to the wrong side. The seam should lie along the edge of the material, slightly over to the wrong side. Fold under a home-made strip 1 cm. Pin and tack the folded edge of the bias binding to the material and remove the pins, turning in or overlapping the ends (unless already seamed together) for finishing.

3 Hem or machine to the material close to the folded and tacked edge. Hem across the end by hand. Remove the tacking.

**To face on to the right side**

1 Start with the facing's right side facing the wrong side of the material, raw edges matching, and join together.

2 Turn the facing to the right side, and turn in the raw edge of the facing. Pin and tack the folded edge of the facing to the material and remove the pins. Hem, or machine the folded edge in place with neat topstitching (see page 57). Remove the tacking and press.

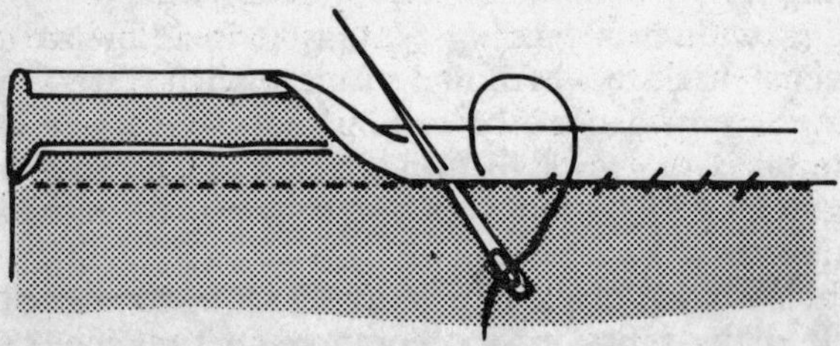

**To mitre the facing corner**

1 Form a diagonal pleat across the corner, matching the fold to the edge of the material. Pin and tack along the diagonal join and remove the pins. Backstitch or machine where tacked and remove the tacking.

2 Trim away the corner fold leaving a 1-cm seam allowance. Press the seam open.

3 When machining the facing to the material, right sides facing, continue round the corner across the seam.

4 When turning the facing to the wrong side, turn over the corner too, and include it in the hemmed edge.

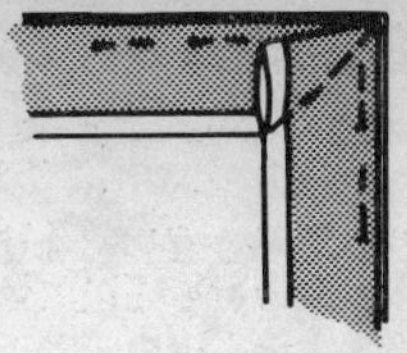

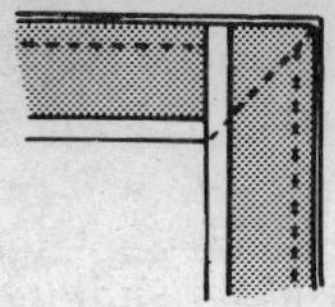

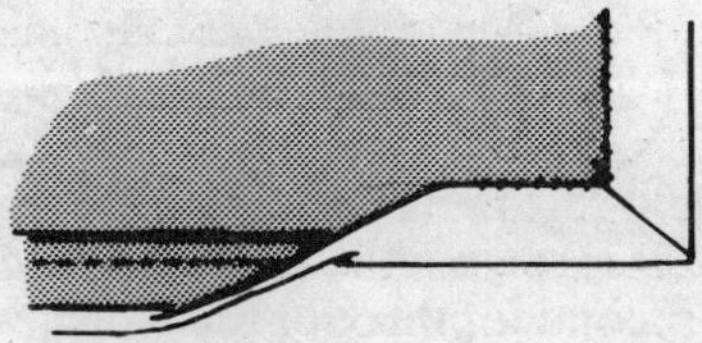

## *Sewing on a button*

First decide where the button is to go and mark the position on the material with a pin or tailor's chalk, or by transferring it from the pattern. (See page 155.)

1 Thread a needle with single or double thread depending on the size of the button, and knot the thread end. For extra thick material use strong button thread.

2 In addition to the knot, secure the thread by one or two small backstitches on the wrong side, then push the needle through from the wrong side at the mark where the button is to go. Pass it through the first hole from the underside of the button and draw the thread through the button.

3 Put the needle back in through the second hole opposite diagonally, and pass it down through the material again. Don't pull the thread too tight. Leave it a little loose to form a shank or stem. Repeat for three stitches through these two holes, then come up through the third hole and cross diagonally to the fourth hole. Repeat for three stitches through these two holes.

4 When the stitches are completed bring the needle up to the surface of the material under the button and wind the thread round the threads securing the button two or three times. Take the needle back to the wrong side and finish off with one or two small backstitches.

*For thick material* place a needle under the stitches, across the top of the button and sew over it. When it is removed there will be extra thread to form a shank to accommodate the thick material from the buttonhole side when fastened.

*A two-hole button* is sewn on in the same way but from one hole to the second for three or four stitches.

*A shank button* is sewn on similarly, but the stitches are taken over the shank.

## Buttonholes

To make a buttonhole you will need a ruler or tape measure, tailor's chalk or a pencil, pins, small needlework or embroidery scissors, a needle, and thread.
1 To mark the position of the buttonhole, transfer the buttonhole placement from the pattern or mark the position yourself.
2 Overlap and pin the buttonhole side over the buttons. Decide whether you are having vertical or horizontal buttonholes or both. To help you: the buttonhole for the neck-edge button under the collar is usually horizontal; so are the ones for cuffs and coat fastenings. Shirt, shirt dress and blouse openings below the neck button are usually vertical. The lowest button is usually at least 6 cm from a blouse hem, and at least 30 cm from a coat hem.
3 To position the buttonholes place them an equal distance from the edge and an equal distance apart. Mark their position with pins on the overlap.
4 Mark the buttonholes by putting a pin down through the centre of the buttonhole position and through the button underneath. Mark the base of the pin on the

overlap with chalk. While in position, feel the edges of the button through the overlap and push a pin down at either side. Mark these pins too with chalk.
5 Remove the pins and join the marks. The buttonhole should be fractionally wider than the button. To make the mark use either pencil, tailor's chalk or a row of small running stitches.
6 Check carefully that the buttonholes do correspond accurately with the buttons, and are in a straight row, equally apart. When you are satisfied that all is correct (and better to make alterations now than make a mistake) take the sharp-pointed scissors and cut a slit starting from the centre of the buttonhole mark. Complete one buttonhole before starting on the next to avoid fraying.
7 Oversew the edges all round first if the material frays easily.
8 Thread the needle with about 30 cm of thread and begin from the left lower end of the buttonhole slit. As well as a knot, backstitch for one or two tiny stitches on the wrong side at this end, then bring the needle through to the right side. Sew round the buttonhole using blanket

*Buttonhole-stitched buttonhole*

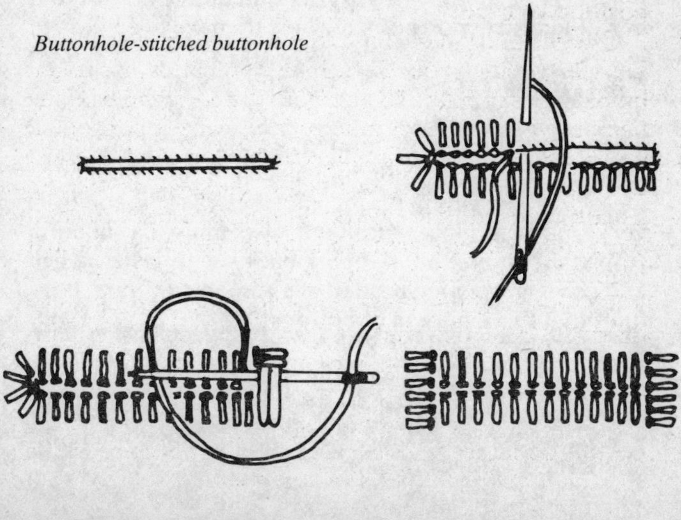

stitch, with stitches an equal length and close together. To achieve this, always bring the needle point back through exactly next to the lower end of the last stitch.

9 When you come to the end of the buttonhole you sew either a round end or a bar end, depending on the type of buttonhole.

(a) A horizontal buttonhole has a round end near the edge of the overlap, and a bar end at the other end.

(b) A vertical buttonhole has two bar or two round ends.

For a *round end* sew a wheel of straight oversewing stitches round the end, always an odd number, say five or seven, with the odd stitch at the middle.

For a *bar end* sew three to five satin stitches across the end of the buttonhole, then blanket stitch (or buttonhole stitch) across them. Continue to blanket stitch along the other side of the buttonhole and at the other end, sew the appropriate round or bar end to finish. Secure the thread with one or two backstitches on the wrong side.

Buttonhole stitch: bring the needle out below the cut. Take the thread behind it and draw the thread through to form a knot on the edge. A machine-stitched buttonhole can be made with zigzag stitches. Consult your machine instruction book for how to make one.

## *Press fasteners*

There are a number of different kinds of press fasteners. Usually they are made of silver- or black-coloured metal, or transparent plastic, and they range in size from very small ones to sew inside the opening of a collar, to stop the corner from flapping back, or to fasten a belt end or waist opening instead of a zipper, to strong, large ones that serve instead of buttons.

**To sew on a press fastener** (see page 46)

1 Overlap the edge where the press fastener is to be sewn, and pin, matching the material design where the edges meet.

2 Mark the position of the press fasteners with tailor's chalk on the overlap, then pass a pin through this mark and mark the pin where it passes into the underlap.
3 Sew on the underside of the press fastener, that is, the side with the knob on it. Start with two or three small backstitches to secure the thread, then oversew through the first hole three times. Take the needle under the material to the next hole and oversew three times through that. Repeat this until you have oversewn through all the holes, then finish off with two or three tiny backstitches. Try to keep the stitches neat and small round the press fastener.
4 Pass a pin through the mark on the overlap through the hole in the centre of the press fastener knob, to check the position. Mark the underside of the overlap where the pin comes through with tailor's chalk, then unpin the overlap.
5 Secure the thread as before with two or three tiny backstitches close to the mark and begin to sew on the upper half. (Once you have got it in position you can check this too, by passing the needle down through the upper and lower half centre holes.) Oversew the upper half in place three times through every hole, but try not to let the stitches show on the right side, by picking up only one layer or just a few threads of the material when stitching. Finish off with two or three small backstitches.

## *Hooks and eyes*

Hooks and eyes are used for securing a waistband overlap on a skirt, or to catch a seam in place above a zipper, or to fasten a quilted jacket down the front, among other things. They come in a range of sizes, from tiny ones to strong versions for skirts. (Special flat hook type fasteners are available for skirts and trousers, too.) You can obtain silver- or black-coloured metal hooks and eyes, and cord-covered large ones for fur or velvet garments.

**To sew on a hook and eye**
The hook is placed under the overlap, with the hook concealed. The eye is placed on the underlap, so that when the hook is fastened into it, it too will be concealed under the overlap. For this reason, it is best to choose 'straight' eyes which can be hidden more easily.

1 Mark the position of the hook and the eye to correspond with it, with pins or tailor's chalk.

2 Sew on the hook using single thread for small hooks and eyes; double thread or button thread for larger sizes. Begin with the hook upper wire ring. Secure the thread with one or two small backstitches then oversew neatly with the smallest stitches possible over the wire ring round to the centre. Take the needle under the material (but not to show on the right side) and oversew the other ring. End by sewing two or three stitches across the straight wires under the hook then finish off with two or three small backstitches.

3 To sew on the eye place it on the underside where marked, and oversew round the first, then the second ring as for the hook, and finish off with one or two small backstitches.

*Underlap* Where a hook is liable to rub against your skin, it is necessary to add a small underlap. Use a small piece of corded petersham ribbon for this, doubled over with the ends turned in and oversewn. Oversew the sides of the ribbon together too. Stitch it to the underlap so it comes beneath the hook and eye when fastened.

## *Sewing in a zipper*

You will need the zipper, a needle, pins, tacking thread, scissors, and the zipper foot for the sewing machine, if available.

The following is the simplest way of sewing in a zipper, in the opening in a plain seam. An open-ended zipper is sewn in in the same way, but from top to bottom of the seam.

1 Tack the plain seam and machine or backstitch below the zipper opening.

2 Open the seam out and press back and finish the seam allowances.

3 With the plain seam and garment (or other item) wrong side uppermost, place the zipper right side against the tacked zipper opening in the seam, with the tag against the material at the top, and the teeth aligned with the tacked seam. The ends of the zipper tapes should be level with the material edge.

4 Pin the zipper tapes right side facing to the seam allowance and garment down each side, starting from the top. Pin first down the left tape, then down the right tape, so that the zipper lies evenly on the seam without rumples.

5 Tack the left-hand zipper tape in place, starting from the top. Use contrasting colour thread, and try to tack in a ruler-straight line, following the woven line down the centre of the zipper tape if there is one. This will act as a tacking guideline, so that when you machine the zipper in place from the right side, you will have the tacking to guide you for straight stitches avoiding the zipper teeth. Tack the right-hand zipper tape from the top in the same way, but at the bottom, turn left and tack below the zipper. Remove the pins.

6 Attach the zipper foot to the sewing machine, adjusted to the left of the needle. Turn the garment right side out. Turn the seam with the zipper tacked to it towards you.

7 Use straight stitching on the machine. Place the left of

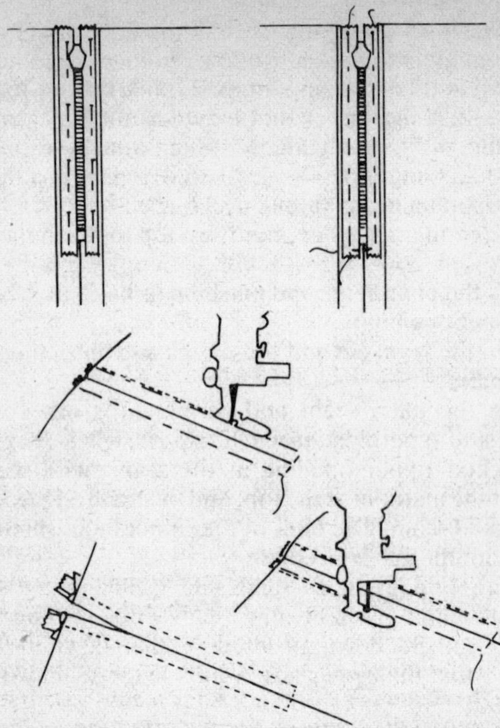

the zipper seam under the machine needle on the stitch-line, close beside the tacking. Machine down to the left of the seam slowly, keeping as straight a stitch row as you can.

Stop at the lower end, raise the zipper foot and pivot towards the centre on the needle. Machine a few stitches to the centre *below* the zipper. Stop machining and take the material back to the beginning for the second tape. Adjust the zipper foot to the right side. Place the right of the zipper seam under the machine needle, and machine down slowly as you did for the left side. At the bottom lift the presser foot and turn on the needle towards the seam and stitch to the centre. Remove the tacking.

8 If the zipper is not being sewn into another seam at the

top, such as a waistband, turn in the ends of the tapes, and hem them to the seam allowance. Do the same with the lower end of the zipper tapes.

The slide fastener should move up and down readily between the two stitchlines. When you have finished sewing in the zipper, change the zipper foot for the general presser foot on the machine.

To sew in a zipper by hand, backstitch from the right side or hem down the wrong side. Supplement the hemming stitches with tiny running stitches.

## *Threading through and joining elastic*

Choose the width of elastic to suit the job it will have to do. Narrow elastic would be enough to gather a hat or sleeves. If it were too wide and strong it could be uncomfortable. But for holding up track-suit trousers you would need medium strong elastic about 1 cm wide. So when buying elastic think about the thickness (called the weight) of the material, and whether the elastic is going to have to support a garment or not. You will need a bodkin or medium-sized safety pin (small enough to pass through the hem or casing). Casing means a strip sewn to material to hold elastic or a tape drawstring.

You will also need scissors, a needle, thread and pins.

1 Tie the elastic round you roughly, to arrive at the approximate length you will need. It should not be too tight but should fit firmly and comfortably. Mark the length with a pin, remove the elastic and cut off the amount you need with a good margin to spare.

2 Slot the end of the elastic through the bodkin or attach the safety pin to one end about 1 cm from the end.

3 Push the bodkin or safety pin into the opening in the hem or casing and begin to pull the elastic through after it. You can feel the bodkin or safety pin through the material. Work your way along pushing the pin or bodkin on through, but be careful not to let the end of the elastic disappear after it or you will have to start again.

4 When the safety pin or bodkin appears at the opening again, pull both the ends of the elastic together, gathering up the material in between. Remove the pin or bodkin and put aside.
5 Adjust the gathered material for a rough fit and tie the ends of the elastic together. If you are sewing elastic into a hem such as a curtain hem, pin the ends of the elastic to the hem at each end instead of tying the ends together.
6 Try on the garment and retie the elastic ends for a really good fit. Trim, leaving about 2.5 cm extra at each end for joining the elastic. Pull several centimetres of the

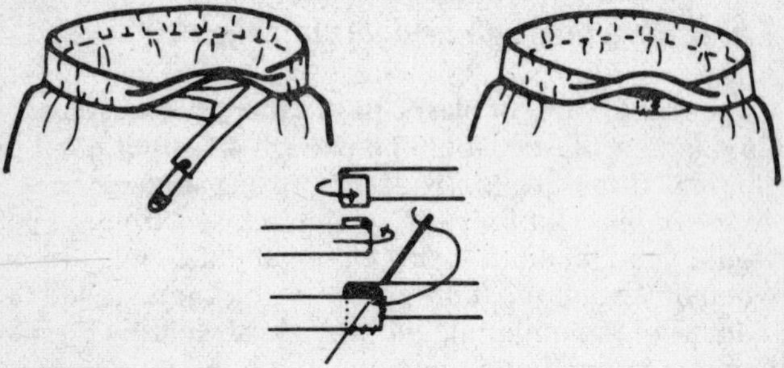

elastic out of the hem or casing at each end to prevent it slipping inside as you join the ends.
7 Thread a needle with double thread and knot the end. Use a thimble if you are able. For the join, the elastic ends are overlapped. Turn under the top elastic 1 cm, and turn over the under elastic 1 cm. Pin the overlapped ends together. Oversew the sides and hem across the width, across each end of the join. Secure with several oversewing stitches.

A drawstring of tape or cord or ribbon is threaded through like elastic, but the ends are tied and left long when worn.

## *To join tape or braid ends*

1 Overlap one end of the tape on to the other. Turn the end which overlaps 1 cm on to the wrong side and pin.

Tack and remove the pins.
2 Turn the end of the underlap on to the right side 1 cm and pin. Tack and remove the pins.
3 Overlap the tape ends 2 to 3 cm and pin together. Tack in place and remove the pins.
4 Using small straight stitches machine the tape overlapped ends together by placing one corner of the overlap under the needle. Machine along one edge. Stop at the corner, pivot on the needle, machine across, pivot at the corner and machine along the lower edge, pivot again and finish machining across the tape to where you began. Remove the tacking and finish off the machine thread ends.

OR

5 By hand, oversew along the upper edge, hem across, oversew the lower edge, then turn the tape wrong side out and hem the other folded end in place. Remove the tacking.

## *Sewing on a tape*

1 Cut the tape to the required length plus 5 cm for turnings.
2 Mark the position where the tape is to be sewn on to the material.
3 Fold the tape end over 1.5 cm on to the *right* side and pin and tack it. Remove the pins.
4 Place the tape end right side against the wrong side of the material where it is to be sewn on. Pin it in place.
5 Tack it in place with small tacking stitches. Remove the pins.
6 Machine it in place with straight stitches along the four sides following the tacking stitches. Remove the tacking.

OR

7 Hem along the top, and oversew the folded end to the material. Oversew the lower edge then turn to the right side and fold the tape back. Oversew the tape and material together along this edge. Remove the tacking.

# Sewing Machines

Sewing machines are very durable, and some people go on using old ones that have been working for fifty years or more, winding the handle to make the machine needle go up and down to make the stitches. Electric sewing machines do the work of operating the needle for you, but the stitches hand machines produce can be just as serviceable. So don't be disappointed if yours is an old-fashioned machine. Provided it stitches well you should be able to get excellent results with it. And that goes for a good toy sewing machine too. (And if you haven't a sewing machine at all, you can sew the way our ancestors did, with a thread and needle, by hand!)

## *Parts of the machine*

Before you begin to use a sewing machine for the first time, it is a good idea to find out what the different parts are for. Opposite is a picture of a hand-sewing machine and an electric one. You will see where they are similar, which is in most important points, and the ways in which they differ.

All machines have a hand wheel (1). A hand machine has a handle too. In the centre of the hand wheel on most sewing machines is a big inner wheel which when turned stops the needle operating, for filling the bobbin. The reel of thread slots on top of the spool pin (2) and the thread is taken across to a guide hook then down round the tension regulator (3) which controls the tautness of the thread going to the needle. Then the thread goes through the take-up lever (4), a metal arm that sticks out from the front of the machine. It continues down the front of the machine through various thread guides and, lastly, is threaded through the needle (5).

Below the machine needle are two rectangular metal plates, in the base of the machine (6). The back one is called the throat plate, and has two rows of teeth in it called the feed dog, and a hole in the centre where the thread goes down. In a modern electric machine this may be a wide hole to cater for the needle moving from side to side for zigzag stitching, and for the left, centre and right choices of position for the needle. In a straight-stitch machine it is usually a small round hole.

The front metal plate, called the slide plate (7), slides open and underneath it you will find the bobbin spool, a

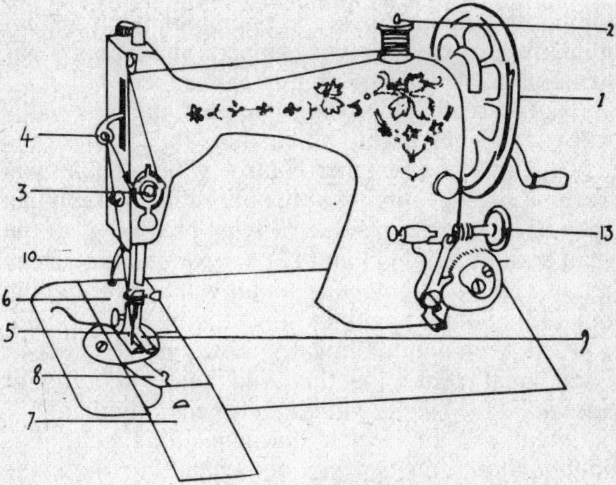


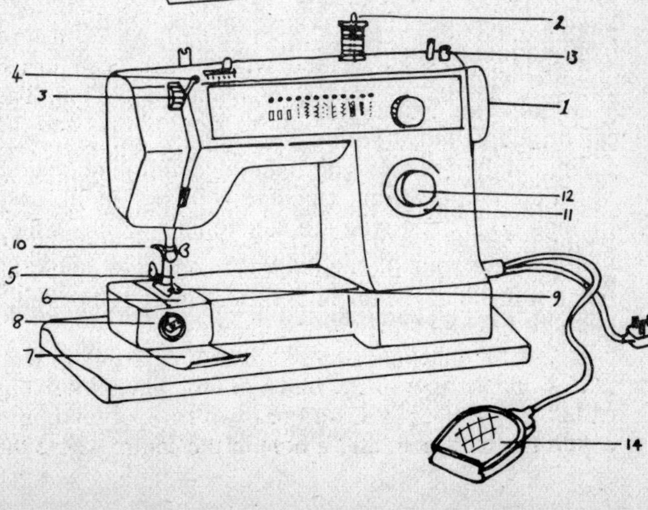

small metal or plastic reel round which you wind the bobbin thread required for the underside of the stitches (8). It sits in the bobbin case. Behind the needle and attached to a post coming down is a metal foot (9). This is called the presser foot. It keeps the material steady while it is passed under the needle, and after sewing is lifted off the material by a springy clip behind the machine called the presser foot lever (10). (In the machine attachments other presser foot types are included, usually one for sewing zippers, and others. Your instruction book will explain how to use them.)

Except on really old sewing machines, there is usually a stitch length regulator, which alters the length of the stitches; and a reverse stitch control, which enables you to reverse straight stitches at the beginning and end of a row to save you the trouble of tying or sewing off the thread ends by hand (11 and 12). On top of the machine there will be a small mechanism for winding the bobbin spool (13). Some machines wind the bobbin in place below the needle automatically. Your instruction book will tell you if yours is like this. And there is a control for pressure on the fabric, which rarely needs altering.

So what will an electric machine do as well? It is labour-saving. You can use both hands to guide the sewing as you machine, because you operate the needle from a foot pedal (14). The treadle machine which you operate with your feet gives you this advantage too. Many of them enable you to sew zigzag stitches which can be adapted to all sorts of sewing jobs, such as sewing machined buttonholes or over-edge finishing seams. More elaborate sewing machines still sew embroidery stitches. The latest type are electronic machines which work by pressing buttons. Many modern machines allow for free-arm sewing. This means the end of the machine can be altered so it is narrow enough to fit inside a sleeve, to enable you to machine all round with ease.

**The instruction book**

Treasure your machine instruction book, because it will

tell you how to use every part of the sewing machine; how to oil it and how to deal with faults.

**Machine needles**

Machine needles push up into the needle bar at one end of the machine. The flat side has to go to the back and the groove in the needle you can feel with your thumbnail, down the front. The needle clamp screw is tightened to hold it in place; loosened to remove it.

Machine needles come in a range of sizes to suit different thicknesses of material. They are coded on the needle and packet. Apart from sharp-pointed needles, ball-point needles are good for sewing knitted material, and wedge-shaped needles are used for sewing leather.

*machine needle sizes (Imperial and metric)*

| | | |
|---|---|---|
| 9 | 65 | for sheer or fine materials such as voile |
| 11 | 80 | for light cotton such as gingham |
| 14 | 90 | for medium materials such as brushed rayon |
| 16 | 100 | for heavier materials such as coat fabric |
| 18 | 110 | for tough materials such as stiff canvas |

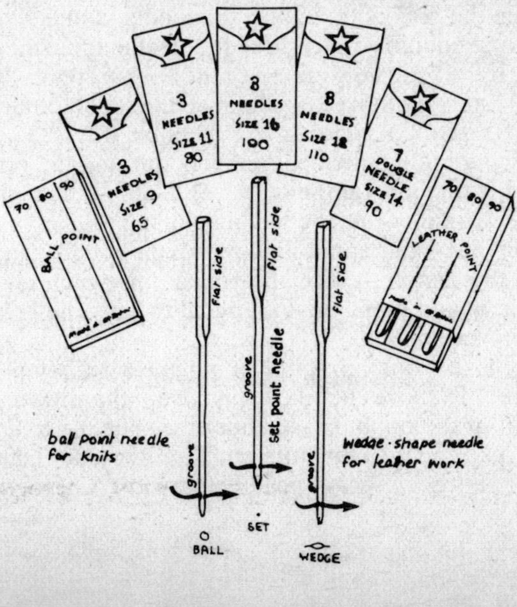

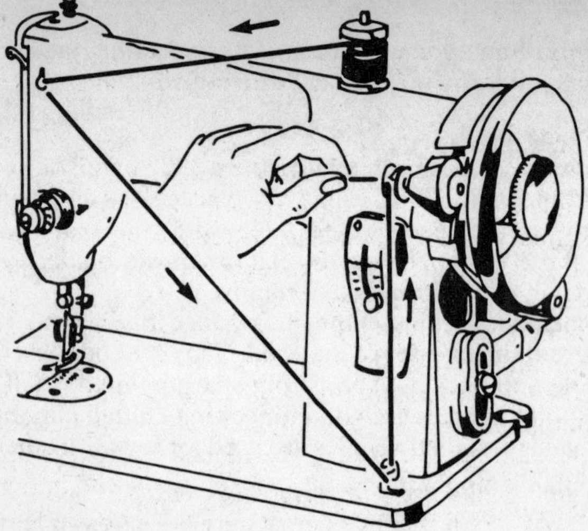

*To thread your sewing machine*

**Wind the bobbin spool first**

Always start with an empty spool from which all old threads have been removed.

1 Place the reel of thread on the spool pin and wind it across the bobbin winder thread guide, then pass the end through the little hole on top of the bobbin spool. Wind the thread two or three times round the spool to start.

2 Clip the bobbin spool on to the bobbin winder.

3 Unwind the hand-wheel screw by turning the centre ring in it forward (anti-clockwise) to stop the machine needle working while the bobbin is filling.

4 Push the bobbin spool clip towards the bobbin winder. Wind the handle, move the treadle or switch on the electricity and press the foot pedal to start the bobbin winder working.

5 When the bobbin spool is fully wound, stop the machine. Remove the filled spool from the winder and place it in the bobbin case under the slide plate. Draw the thread end into the little groove at the side. Tighten the hand-wheel screw again clockwise. *Check these*

*points against your own machine instruction book in case yours is different. If so, follow your book's instructions.*

**To thread the needle**

Place the reel of thread on the spool pin and draw the thread along the top of the machine. Pass the thread over the guide and down between the tension regulator discs; up again through the take-up lever and down through the thread guides on the way to the needle. Trim the thread and pass it through the needle from front to back.

**To draw up the bobbin thread**

1 With the slide plate open, take hold of the hand wheel at the side and lower the threaded machine needle down into the bobbin. Draw the needle up again with the hand wheel. When it comes up through the hole in the throat

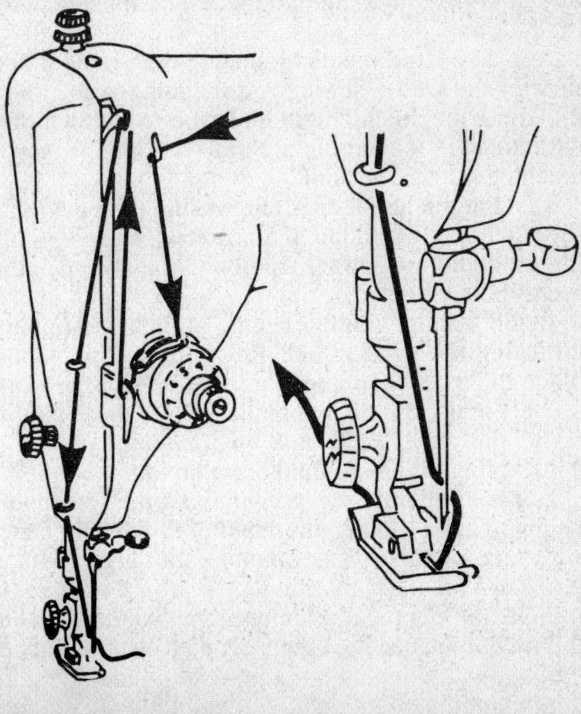

plate there should be a loop round the needle thread, made of the bobbin thread.
2 Take a sewing needle and pick up the loop and hook it out. The bobbin thread will emerge. Draw the bobbin and needle threads together back through the presser foot and trim to about 10 cm. Close the slide plate.

## *Using the sewing machine*

It helps, if the machine is not in its own steady cabinet, to have it on a firm table in a good light. The table should be clean and clear except for your sewing and the tools you'll be using. Have your small scissors handy.

Sit at the table on a comfortable, hardback chair at the right height. Switch an electric machine off when you are adjusting the attachments, and immediately if it gets hot or smokes! If anything like this ever happens, pull out the plug too.
1 Add any attachments or change the needle if necessary for the kind of sewing you are going to do.
2 Adjust the stitch length and type to that which you wish to use. If yours is a zigzag machine, follow the machine instruction book.
3 Test the stitches. Every time you use the machine, test the stitches on an oddment of material, preferably of the material you are sewing, so you can make any adjustments before you begin.
4 Begin sewing with the needle at its highest point by adjusting the hand wheel. Raise the presser foot and place the stitchline under the needle, with the work to the left of the needle if possible. Lower the presser foot on to the material. Switch on if necessary, when the light, if there is one, should come on too.

Begin to operate the machine and the stitchline will begin to travel under the needle. Guide the material without pushing or pulling it under the needle, with your left hand for hand machining, or with both hands for treadle and electric machining. Keep your fingers out of the way of the needle, especially with electric machines.

**For straight stitchlines**

To get a straight stitchline you need a guide to follow to help you not to waver, like using a ruler when drawing a straight line. On a machine, you can do this by keeping the edge of the material parallel with a guide as you sew, which, as the needle is a fixed point away, will produce the straight line you're aiming at. You can do this in any of the following ways.

1 Follow the inside or outside edge of the presser foot. This is a reliable way of forming a straight stitchline, but it will be fairly near the edge of the material.

2 Follow one of the engraved guidelines on the throat plate.

3 Follow a hem or seam guide screwed into the machine bed, with the end adjusted against the material (see your instruction book).

4 A magnetic seam guide can be fixed to the metal machine where it will rest against the edge of the material as it moves under the needle, keeping it moving straight along.

A straight row of stitches on the right side of the material for decoration is called *topstitching*.

**Machining round corners**

If you come to a corner, stop, raise the presser foot, but leave the needle down through the material. Pivot the material on the needle to turn the corner for the following stitchline. Lower the presser foot again and continue machining.

Machine round curves slowly, guiding the material gently to follow the curve round without piling up past the needle.

**Machining thick material or thick seams**

Trim away corners and layers of seam allowance at seam junctions on heavyweight fabric. Even so, the machine may find it difficult to cope with very thick parts. Don't force it. It is better to stop, and sew across the thick part by hand. Backstitch looks very like machine straight stitch, so you could use this on thick material.

**Starting and finishing off machine stitching**

1 Reverse stitch for a few stitches at the beginning and end of straight stitch rows.

2 Sew or tie off the thread ends. First pull the thread end on the wrong side of the material and a little loop of thread will show from the other side. Put a needle under this loop and pull the thread through to the wrong side. Trim the threads and thread them into a darner. Sew them off with two or three small backstitches, or tie them together and snip the ends.

**Machine stitch faults**

Breaking needles? Skipped stitches? Breaking thread? The machine won't sew?

1 Make sure it is correctly threaded by starting again threading carefully, instruction book in hand.

2 Check the thread isn't caught up somewhere, such as in the bobbin or round the spool pin. Switch off an electric machine before poking round in it for loose threads.

3 Reset or change the needle. It may be loose or blunt. If it is broken, be sure you rescue the broken tip too. Switch off the electricity before changing the needle.

4 Unsatisfactory stitches – if the stitches are too tight on top and looped underneath, or too loose on top and tight below, you have probably got a problem with the thread tension. Ask a grown-up to help you adjust this, as it can be tricky. The instruction book will tell you how with diagrams.

A sewing machine needs regular oiling with fine sewing machine oil, as directed in the instruction book. And it needs regular servicing, too, at a sewing machine shop, just like a motor car at a garage.

# Pressing Your Sewing

Part of sewing things successfully is to make them look as well finished as you can – the way the garment manufacturer would. He always sees that clothes are carefully pressed before being sent to the shop.

While you are in the process of making something, if you press as you go, the sewing will look tidy and it will help you to judge the effect more easily, and see the next step more clearly.

You will need an electric iron and an ironing board. You will also need some pieces torn from an old cotton sheet measuring about 60 cm square, or you can buy press cloths. These are for damp pressing, or covering delicate material for dry pressing. A steam iron also damp presses for you: refer to the instruction leaflet if you are using one of these.

There are other items of pressing equipment: tailor's hams, hard cushions in various shapes for pressing over; a padded glove called a pressing mitt, for ironing puff sleeves; a velvet pressing board, though a rough towel with the velvet right side against it, lightly pressed on the wrong side, makes a good alternative. A sleeve board can be very useful for ironing sleeves.

## *Controlling the iron's heat*

Materials vary in the amount of heat they can stand without damage when being ironed. Synthetic materials like nylon melt under strong heat, so a cool iron is required for them. Cotton, on the other hand, needs a very hot iron. So you will need to adjust the iron's heat to suit your material, and if it's a mixture of synthetic and natural fibres, to suit the one which needs the lesser heat. For instance, for material made of cotton and nylon, you would have to adjust the iron to the setting required for pressing nylon, or you could damage the fabric.

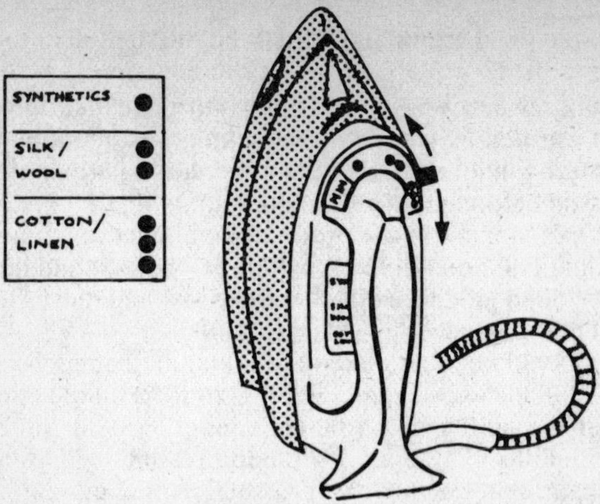


**Adjusting the iron's heat**
On the iron you will usually see a dial marked with words or symbols, which you set opposite the setting arrow.

| *words* | *symbol* | *material* |
|---|---|---|
| cool | 1 dot | synthetic materials; silky rayon |
| warm<br>medium hot | 2 dots | silk; silky materials<br>wool dry ironed; heavy cotton-style rayon; light cotton such as voile or lawn |
| hot<br>very hot | 3 dots | wool, damp-pressed under a press cloth; damp cotton; cotton; linen |

## *Pressing*

1 Press the length of material before you begin cutting out, if it is crumpled.
2 When cutting out, press any creased or crumpled shapes before tacking.
3 After sewing, press seams and darts and other construction details such as collars and cuffs. Press the seams open on the wrong side; press the darts to one

side, and press seams and darts from the right side, too.
4 On a dress or skirt, press the whole garment before turning up the hem. When you have turned up and tacked the hem, press the folded edge only. When finally pressing a hem, don't take the iron over the taped or hemmed edge, because this would make it show up as a ridge on the right side.
5 When your work is completed, press it all over, and inspect it for any loose threads or tacking left in. Hang it up on a hanger or fold it away carefully in a clean plastic carrier bag.

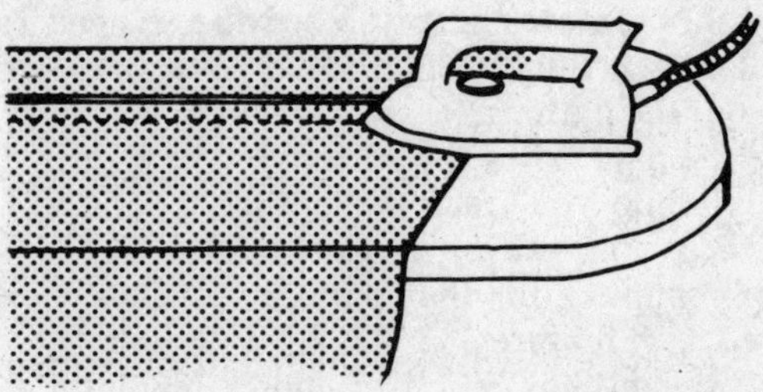

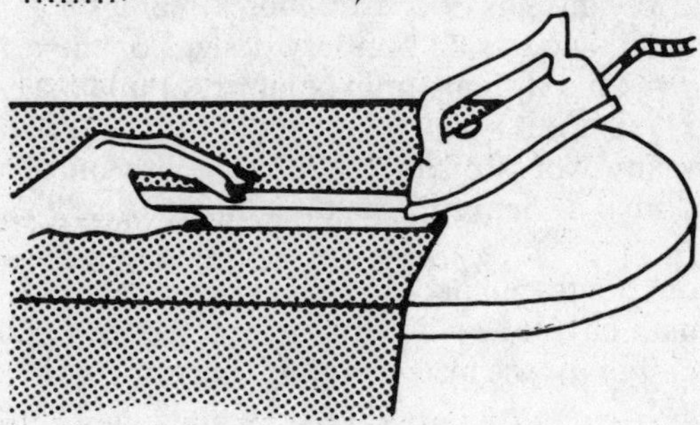

# To Make Your Own Patterns From This Book

## *Traced patterns*

Some patterns in this book are drawn on the page full size for you to trace, and with some of the chart patterns, parts may be drawn full size, such as the mouse's ear on page 125. You will need to trace those, too.

Tracing paper is thin paper you can see through. Greaseproof paper is ideal for this and easy to obtain. There may be some in the kitchen, so ask if you may have a sheet or two. Or you can buy it from hardware or grocers' shops, quite cheaply. You will also need a ruler, a pencil or felt-tip pen, and some general scissors for cutting out the pattern.

1 Place the paper over the pattern on the page and hold it steady while you trace the outline carefully. Use a ruler to help you with any straight lines.

2 Trace shapes on the pattern separately where indicated: e.g. features.

3 Trace any designs or construction symbols on to your pattern too, such as embroidery designs or the arrows which mark the straight grain of fabric, or fold edge (see page 151) symbols.

4 Copy any words on the printed pattern on to your tracing, such as 'leave open for stuffing' or 'sew ear on here'.

5 Cut out the traced pattern shapes separately and store them in an envelope with the name of the item and the page number for the instructions for making it written on the outside.

## *Making a full-size pattern from a chart*

These charts are drawn to the scale: 1 square = 5 cm. This is the size of metricated squared dressmaking paper, which is drawn in centimetres with bold 5-cm square larger divisions.

If you can get hold of squared dressmaking paper, bought from the haberdashery department in stores, or at large stationers, it will make the job of enlarging the pattern easier. Otherwise take a large sheet of newspaper, brown paper or wallpaper lining paper, and mark along the edges every 5 cm. Join the marks with a ruler and felt-tip pen or pencil, to make 5-cm squares.

1 Draw the outline of the chart full size on the 5-cm squared paper.

2 Number the sides of the outline to match the numbers on the chart.

3 *Copy the pattern shapes full size from the chart. To do this, place a dot on the line wherever a pattern shape crosses it, looking at the number at the top and the side of the chart at this point to give you your bearings (like reading a map). Place the dot on the full-size pattern line as near to the same place as you can. Continue until you have completed the outline dots, then join them together.

4 Copy the words and symbols on the chart on to the full-size pattern, and write any other information on a piece of paper to keep with it for reference.

5 Cut out the pattern and store it in a large envelope with the name and page number of the item written on the front.

## *Measuring yourself*

For making clothes that will fit you, you are going to need to note your measurements, to compare with the pattern, or with the garment while you are making it. For instance, when making a skirt, you will need to know your waist size, for cutting out the waistband, and you'll need to know the finished length for a sleeve, or a dress. Overleaf is a list of useful personal measurements for dressmaking. Before you start, have a tape measure, a

*Sometimes to make a larger or smaller size you may have to add or take away an amount from the full-size pattern, such as for the track suit. The chart will tell you how and where.

piece of paper or a postcard, and a pencil or pen ready.

To take a measurement, place the end of the tape marked 1 at the beginning, and hold it there firmly, then take the tape to the other end of the measurement, such as from the neck to the waist, and read the number there. This number is the one to note down. You may need a helper for taking back measurements. For measurements round the body, start at the beginning and bring the tape round and overlap the end. Pinch the tape together at this point and the number where the tape overlaps its end will give you the measurement.

**Measurements list**

*chest* – bust if your figure is developing:
(*taken round fullest point of chest*)
*waist*:
(*take tape round waist snugly*)
*hips*:
(*take the tape round the widest part of the hips, slightly up in front*)
*back waist length*:
(*from the prominent bone at the base of the neck to the waistline*)
*shoulder*:
(*from base of neck to the shoulder joint*)
*arm length*:
(*from shoulder joint to wrist with arm bent*)
*arm circumference*:
(*taken round upper arm*)
*wrist circumference*:
(*taken round wrist, not too tightly*)
*neck circumference*:
(*taken round neck, not too tightly*)
*finished skirt length*:
(*from back waist to the desired finished skirt length*)
*finished dress length*:
(*from the base of the neck to the desired finished dress length*)

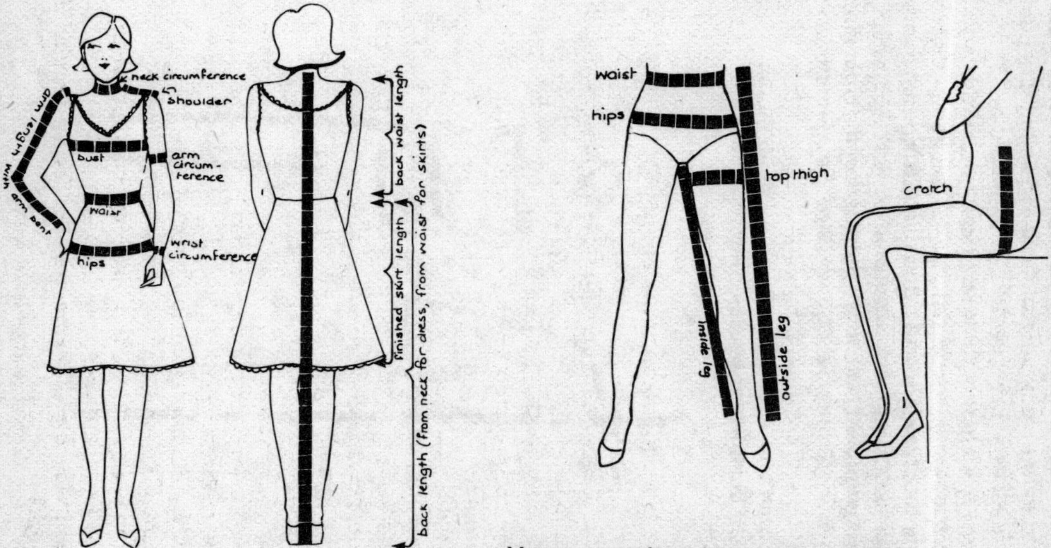


*Measurements for girls' and ladies' clothes*

***trousers***
*waist size*:
(*as above*)
*outside leg length*:
(*from waist to desired finished trousers length*)
*inside leg length*:
(*from crotch to lower end of trousers leg inside the leg*)
*crotch*:
(*from waist to chair seat when sitting down: see chart*)
*crotch seams (girls and women)*:
(*it is a good idea to measure the length of the crotch seams on a pair of trousers that fit you well, for comparison with the ones you are making*)
*top thigh*:
(*round thigh where shown*)

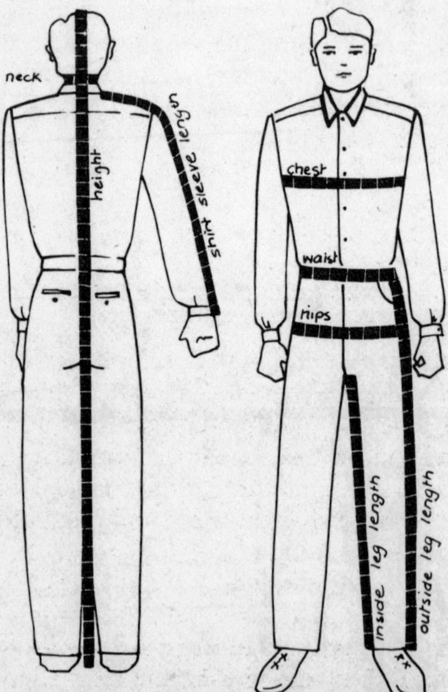


*Measurements for boys' and men's clothes*

# Projects

## *Butterfly needlebook*

Here is a pretty and useful needlebook you can make to begin with, for practice in tracing a pattern, cutting out, tacking and backstitch. You will then have something to store your needles in.

**You will need**

For each butterfly shape:
15-cm wide × 10-cm long felt (for two shapes for the needlebook, one 23-cm square of felt would be enough)
tacking or sewing thread
embroidery thread

**Pattern**
Trace the pattern shape from the next page and cut out on the fold of the material.

**To cut out**
Pin the pattern on the folded felt for the first shape (and for the first colour if you are using different coloured felt for each). Use the medium-size scissors and cut carefully round the pattern. Remove the pins and pin the pattern to the felt again, or to the second colour felt, and cut out the second shape. Unpin and return the pattern to its envelope.

**To make**
1 Place the felt shapes together matching the edges, and pin together lightly to prevent them from slipping.
2 Tack together across close to the centre. Remove pins.

3 Thread the embroidery needle with embroidery thread and knot the thread end. Backstitch the shapes together down the centre. Remove the tacking. Use the needlebook folded like a book, or open flat.

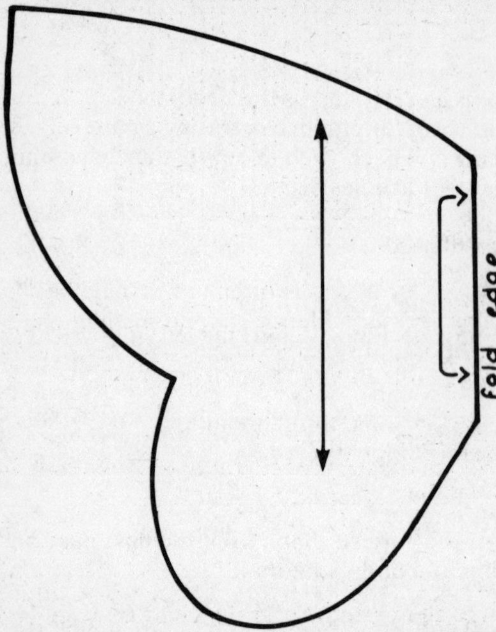


½ shape – cut on folded material

## *Butcher's apron*

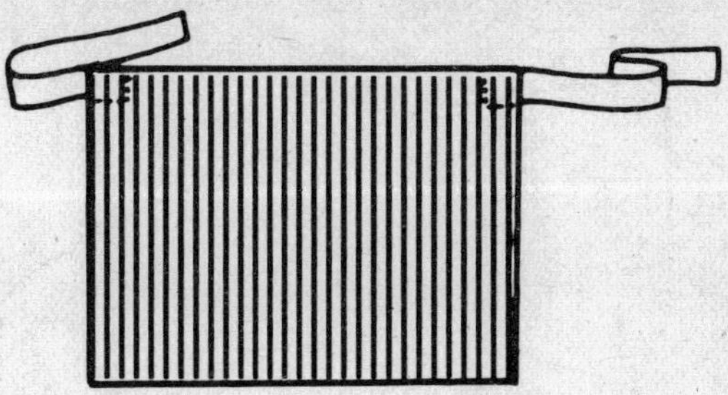

A present for a man is often a problem. This butcher's apron is very easy to make and would be a useful gift. If you cannot find suitable striped material, strong, plain-coloured cotton would be equally good.

**You will need**

75 cm of 90-cm wide cotton (or wider if wished)
2 metres of tape 2.5 cm wide
thread

**Pattern**

Enlarge the pattern from the chart on page 70 and cut out.

**To cut out**

First fold the material together from side to side, and pin the selvages together to make sure the shape is true. Trim and pull into shape to form an exact rectangle. Fold the material ready to cut out the apron as shown in the diagram (for 90-cm wide material use the 75-cm length as it is). Pin the pattern to the folded material, matching the fold edge of the pattern to the fold edge of the material. Cut out the apron, but not along the fold. Unpin and put the pattern away.

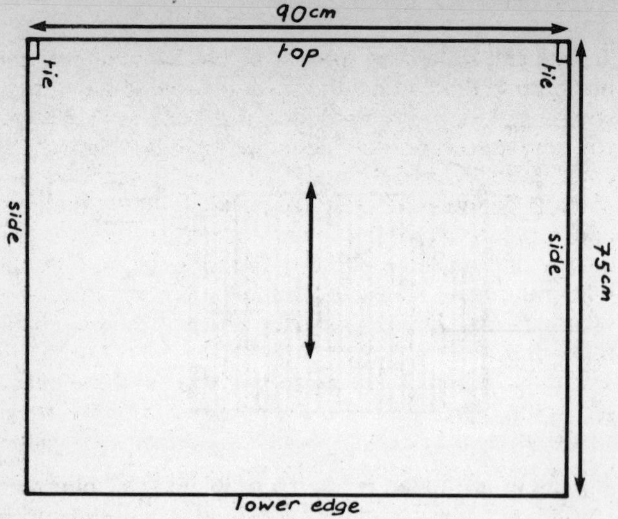


**To make**

1 Thread the needle and knot the thread. Turn a 1-cm wide hem down each side of the material. If the sides are woven selvages a single hem turning will be enough. When you turn over the hems the stripes should align as shown in the diagram, both lengthwise and crosswise.

2 Turn a 1-cm wide hem along the top and lower edges. Pin and tack.

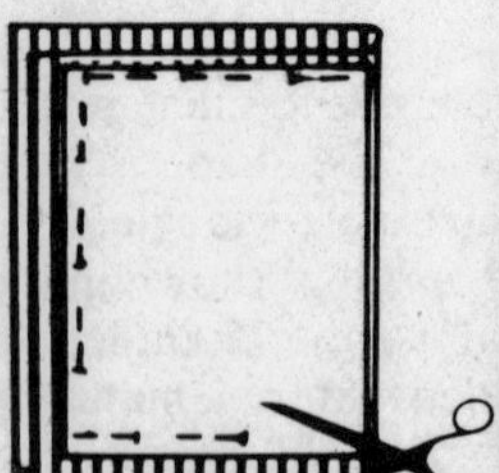

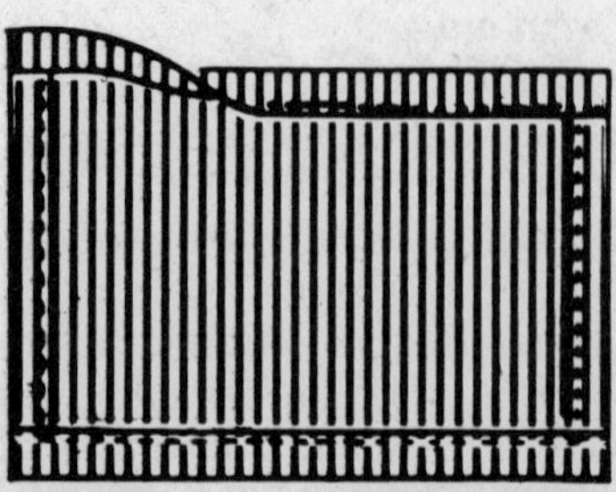

3 Reverse for a few stitches at the beginning of the machining, then adjust the sewing machine for straight stitching. Use the presser foot as a guide for a straight row and machine stitch along the top edge. Stop at the corner and pivot on the needle. Start again and continue machining down the side. Turn again at the next corner and machine along the lower edge, then turn the last corner and machine along the other side, back to the beginning again. Reverse for a few stitches at the end of the machining. If sewing by hand, hem all the way round the apron.

4 Cut two tapes, each 1 metre long. Turn in the ends and pin to the corners of the apron at the waist on the wrong side where marked on the pattern. Sew on, following the instructions for sewing on tape (see page 49).

5 Remove the tacking and press the apron.

The apron is worn with the tapes crossed at the back and tied at the front.

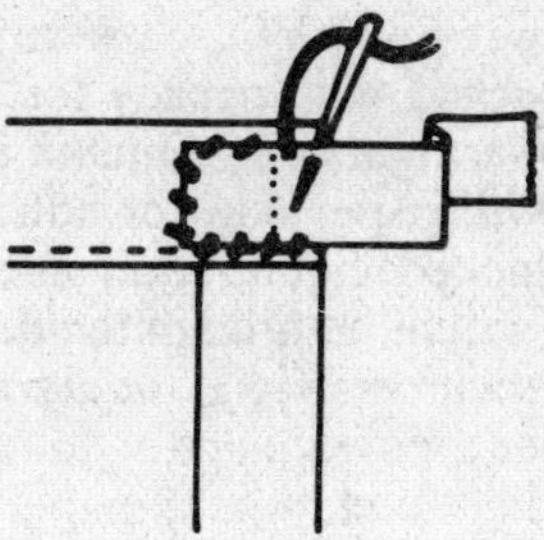

## *PVC apron*

This apron is made out of PVC, plastic-coated sponge-able material, but you could make it out of woven cotton material instead. You would need to make similar hems to the butcher's apron (page 69) if so. PVC needs only single hems, because the plastic surface will not fray at the edges.

Pin marks show up on PVC, so where possible it is best to secure the turned edges ready for machining (and machining with straight, long stitches is preferable for this material) with paper clips or adhesive tape. PVC seams can be tacked in the seam allowance, but not hems. You can machine through the adhesive tape and strip if off afterwards, but it would be necessary to remove the paper clips as you go or you risk breaking the machine's needle. Tack where paper clips and tape won't work.

**You will need**

75 cm of 60-cm wide lightweight PVC. (65 cm of 50-cm long × 50-cm wide material

1.6 metres of 2.5-cm wide twill braid or tape

thread

**Pattern**

Copy the pattern shape full size on squared paper (see page 62) and cut out.

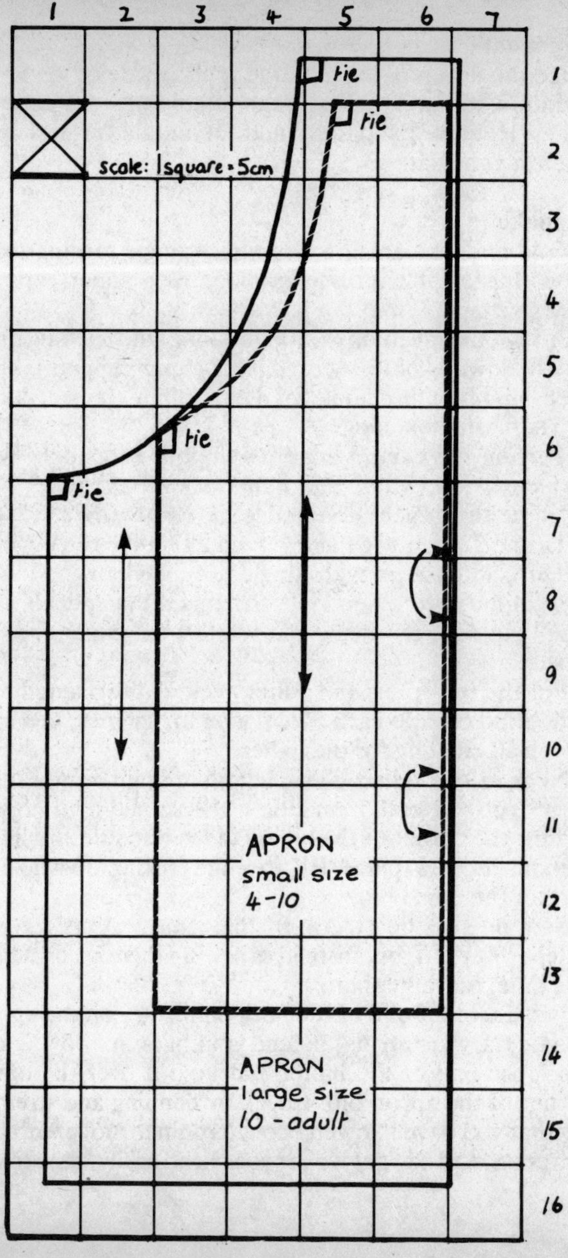
1 2 3 4 5 6 7
1 2 3 4 5 6 7 8 9 10 11 12 13 14 15 16
tie
tie
scale: 1 square = 5cm
tie
tie
APRON
small size
4-10
APRON
large size
10 - adult

**To cut out**

Place the apron pattern on the reverse side of the PVC and draw round it, using a ruler to help with the straight edges. Remove the pattern and cut out the apron shape. Put away the pattern.

**To make**

1 Fold over the apron sides with a single turning 1 cm wide. Fasten the turning in place with paper clips or adhesive tape.

2 Adjust the machine to straight, long stitches. Machine slowly down each turned edge, if paper-clipped taking each clip off in turn ahead of the stitchline. If using tape, rip it off after stitching.

3 Turn in the curved edges of the bib in a single hem 0.75 cm wide. Tack this hem without pinning, then machine along each curved edge and remove the tacking.

4 Turn a 2.5-cm wide single hem along the top edge of the bib, and a 1-cm wide single turning along the lower edge of the apron. Secure both hems with paper clips or tape. Machine the hems and remove the paper clips or tape.

5 For the tie strings and halter neck, cut two lengths of twill braid or tape each 50 cm long for the ties, and one length 60 cm long for the halter.

6 Neck halter: take a 60-cm length of braid or tape, and turn over one end 1 cm. Place the turned-over corner against the corner of the bib on the wrong side and tack, then machine, in place. Remove the tacking. Just do one end for the time being.

7 Sew on two tie strings in the same way as for the butcher's apron, but instead of sewing them on by hand, this time, machine them.

8 For the other end of the neck halter: try on the apron and tie the waist strings behind your back in a bow. Take the loose end of the halter and hold it over the other corner of the apron bib. Check by bending and stretching that you have allowed enough room to move with the halter on, and can get it over your head easily, then mark

where the braid or tape meets the apron bib.

9 Remove the apron and add 4 cm below the marker pin for the overlap. Cut off here, and turn in this end of the halter 1 cm. Tack and machine to the other side of the apron bib as with the other end. Remove the tacking.

10 Press the halter and tie strings but not the PVC. If you have made the apron from cotton material, you can press the finished garment.

## *Sun dress and sun hat*

This sun dress is easy to make and fit. It has side-opening slits in the skirt and shoulder tie strings, and is elasticated round the top and waist. The frilly, lace-edged sun hat is elasticated too, and can be made to match or as a separate item. For fun we made the shoulder ties in a matching, but different-coloured cotton print. The pattern would fit an average-size 10- to 12-year-old.

**You will need**

*Sun dress and sun hat together:*
(allow extra material for larger sizes)

one colour:

- 2 metres of 90-cm wide material (printed cotton, lawn, cotton jersey or stretch terry. Refer to sewing knits for the last two, on page 16.)

two colours:

- 1.5 metres of 90-cm wide material in the main colour
- 50 cm of 90-cm wide material in the second colour
- 2 metres light elastic
- 2 metres bias binding for elastic casing 12 mm (½ in) wide. If you decide to make the shoulder ties from bias binding you would need an additional 2 metres.

2 metres of 3-cm wide lace trimming (or narrower if wished)
thread to match main material, and second colour material if used

*Sun hat only:*

50-cm long × 50-cm wide material
2 metres lace trimming
1 metre light elastic
matching thread

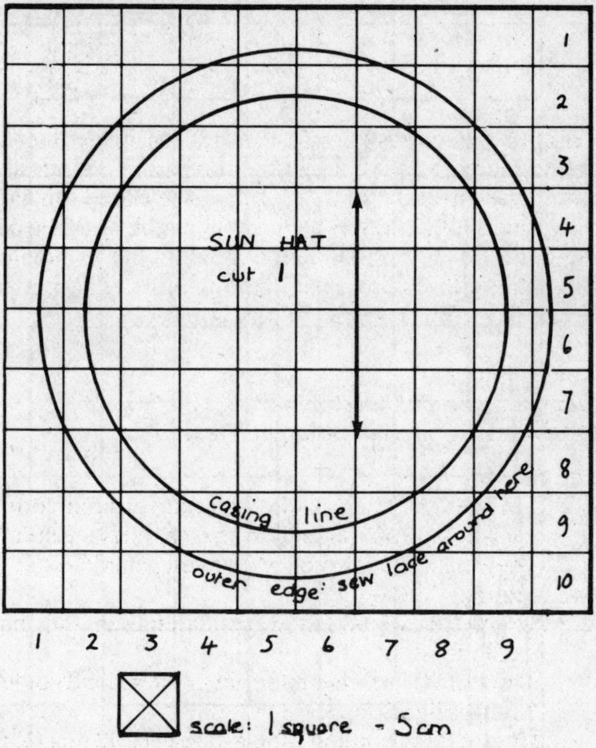

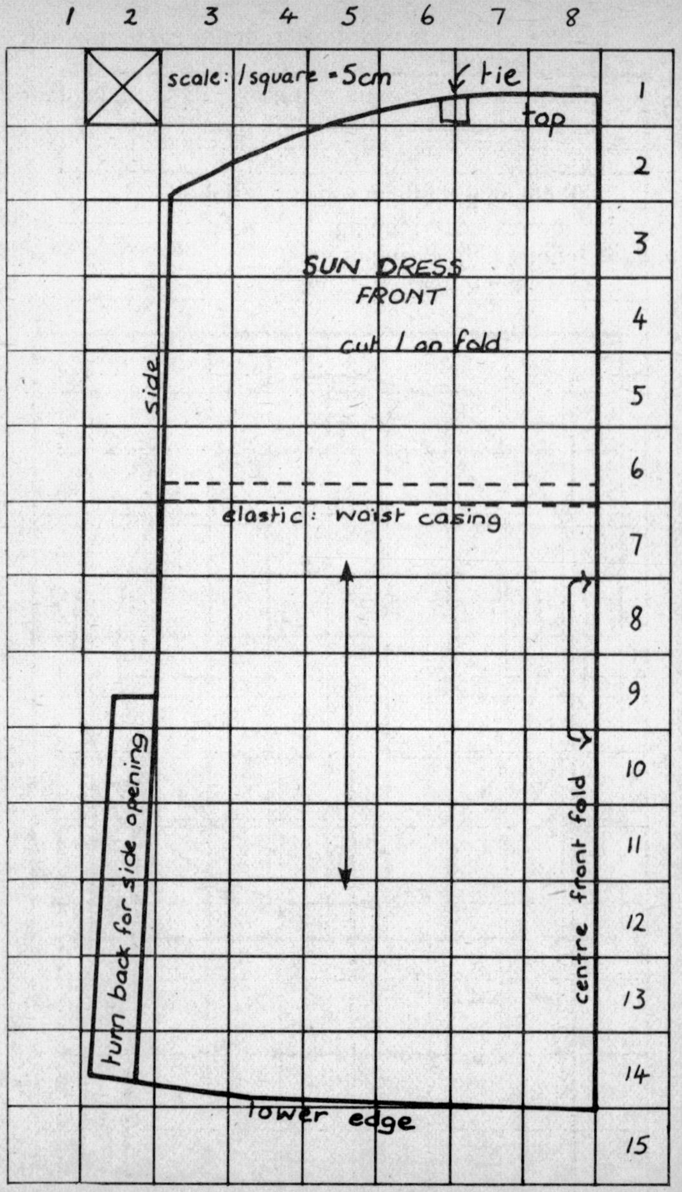

1 2 3 4 5 6 7 8
scale: 1 square = 5cm
tie
top
SUN DRESS
FRONT
cut 1 on fold
side
elastic: waist casing
turn back for side opening
centre front fold
lower edge
1 2 3 4 5 6 7 8 9 10 11 12 13 14 15

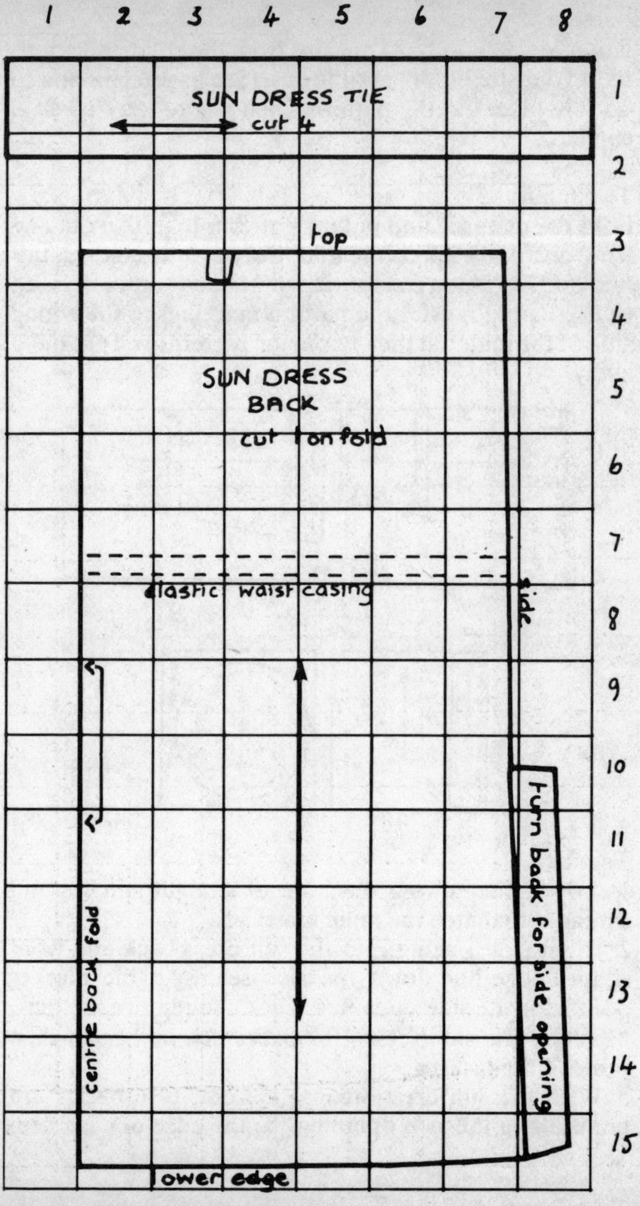

1 2 3 4 5 6 7 8
1 2 3 4 5 6 7 8 9 10 11 12 13 14 15
SUN DRESS TIE
cut 4
top
SUN DRESS
BACK
cut 1 on fold
elastic waist casing
side
turn back for side opening
centre back fold
lower edge

## Pattern

Enlarge the pattern to full size from the chart and adjust to fit your size before cutting out. (See page 62 for how to do this.) Cut out the pattern when you're satisfied all is correct.

## To cut out

Fold the material and pin the patterns to it. Cut out one front and one back on the fold. Cut out four sundress ties and one sun hat in contrasting material if you've decided to use that. Transfer the pattern markings to the wrong side of the material then unpin the patterns and put them away.

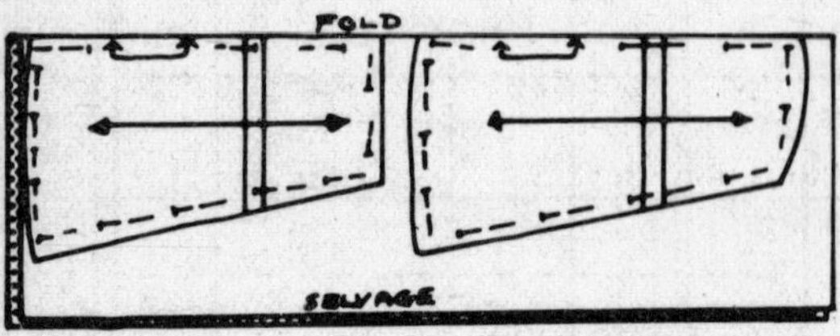


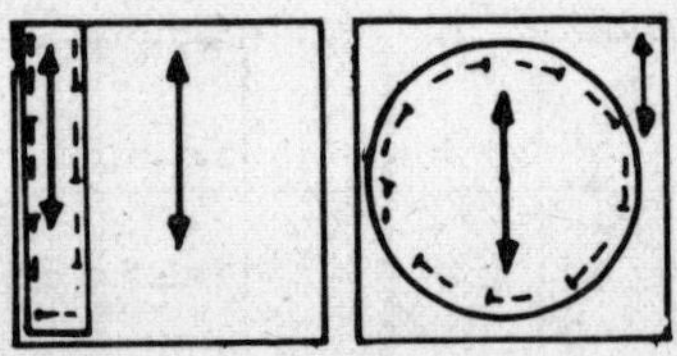

## To make

1 Adjust the sewing machine to straight stitches and thread it to match the main material.

2 Right sides facing, pin the sun dress back and front shapes together down the side seams to the marker points for the side openings. Tack and remove the pins. Machine the side seams (or backstitch by hand), then remove the tacking.

3 With the sun dress wrong side out, turn back 2-cm hems along the side openings, so the edge of each hem

corresponds with the seam line. Pin and tack the hems, then remove the pins, and machine them or hem by hand.

4 Turn 2-cm wide hems along the skirt front and back lower edges. Pin, tack and machine or hem in the same way.

5 Still with the sun dress wrong side out, turn over the top edge for a 2-cm wide hem all round the top. When you are pinning, you will find that the hem on the curved shape will need a small pleat in the folded-under edge to make it lie flat. Make a 0.5-cm pleat at each side about 10 cm from the side seam in the hem at the front. Tack all round and remove the pins.

6 Machine the top hem, stitching round close to where it is tacked, but leave a 2-cm long opening where you begin at the side seam, for threading the elastic through. Machine a second row 0.75 cm above the first row. This will form the frill when elasticated. Press the sun dress.

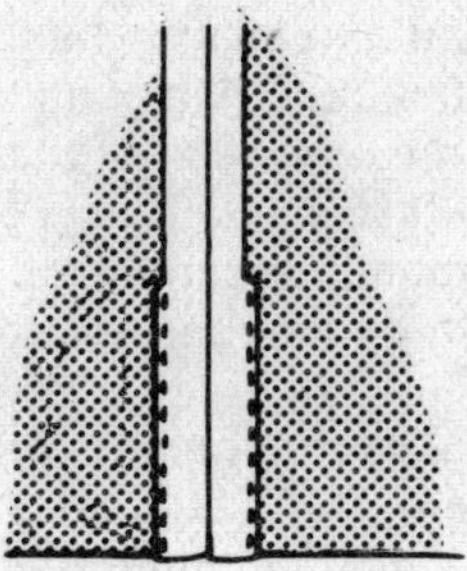

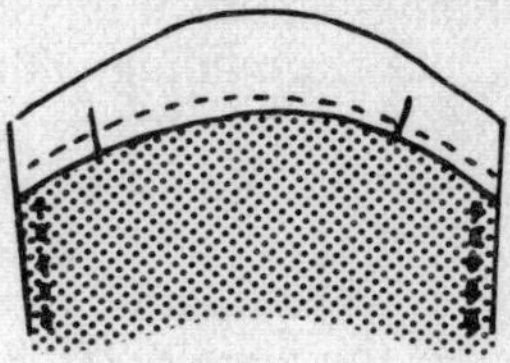

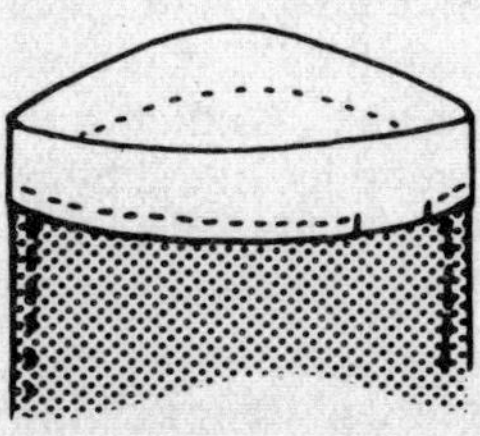

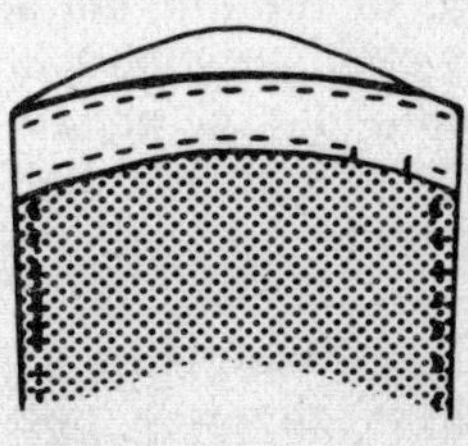

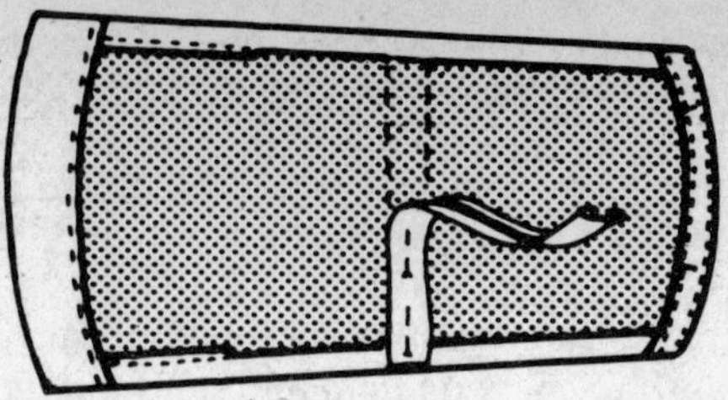

7 Use bias binding for the waistline casing. Turn in the end of the bias binding 1 cm and machine across it. With the sun dress wrong side out, place the end of the bias binding, wrong sides facing, on the transferred pattern mark for the casing – a line round the sun dress waist.

With the bias binding edges still folded in, pin it flat to the dress through the front only, along the casing line. When you reach the side seam, turn the sun dress over, and continue pinning along the back in the same way. At the side seam, first check that the binding is level, and not too tight on the material, then cut the end with 1 cm to spare to turn in. Unpin for a few centimetres and machine across this end to match the other end of the binding. Afterwards, pin the end back again.

Tack the binding to the dress all round. Be careful not to catch the other side of the dress in with the stitches as you do this. Remove the pins.

Open the dress from the top as wide as you can, to slip the casing stitchline along the edge of the bias binding under the needle. (If yours is a free-arm machine, you can use it for this job.) Slowly and carefully stitch the edge of the binding along the top, all round the sun dress. When you've done this, draw the sun dress out from under the needle and snip the threads, then start again, and reposition it with the lower edge of the binding under the needle. Machine all round along this edge. Remove the tacking.

8 The shoulder ties are made by a method called *rouleau*, that is, a tube of material turned right side out to form a tie or drawstring. It's quite fun to do.

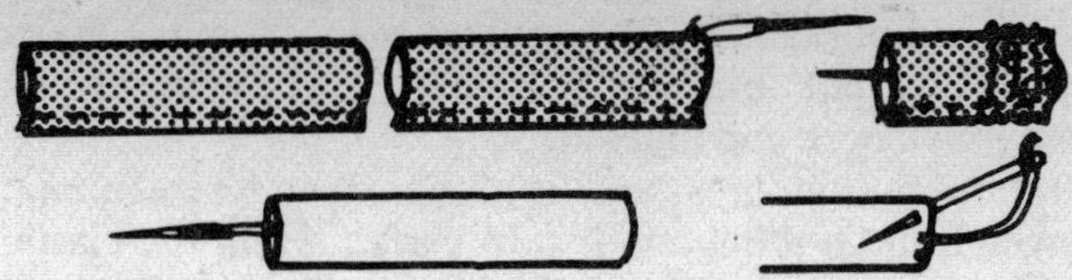

(a) Take the first strip of material and with right sides facing, fold it in half from side to side and pin the edges together. Tack and remove the pins. Machine with a 1-cm seam allowance, then remove the tacking. Repeat for the other three shoulder ties.
(b) Take a short, strong needle such as a tapestry needle, thread it with double thread and knot the thread end. Oversew the thread to one end of a tie strip, but do not snip the thread.
(c) Push the needle into the tube of material, like threading elastic through, and push it along inside, pulling the tube inside after it. The tube will ruche up at first, but as you get the needle through half-way it will easily slip through. You end up with the tube the right side out. Trim 0.25 cm from the end and the needle's thread with it. Re-thread the needle and repeat for the other three ties.
(d) Turn in one end of a tie, and oversew the back and front together. Do the same for the other end and repeat for the other three ties.
(e) Pin the ties to the wrong side of the top of the sun dress where marked from the pattern. Tack and remove the pins. Hem the end of the ties to the sun dress hem, and machine or backstitch across over the upper stitch-line to secure each one firmly.

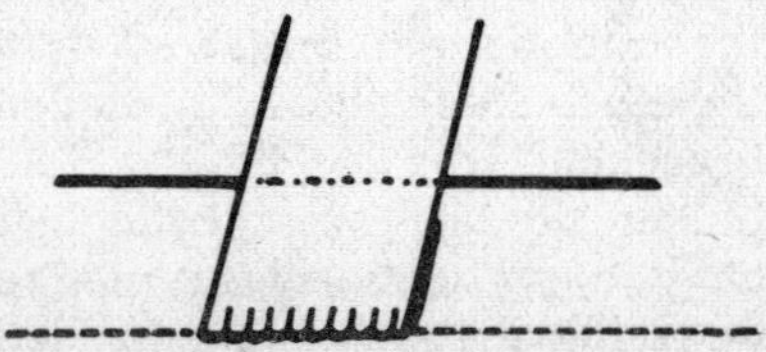

Instead of material, you can use bias binding to make tie strings, cut to the same length, and folded in two along its length and machined.
(f) Press the sun dress and tie strings, then thread elastic through the top hem and waist casing. Hem the elastic openings to close when finished.

**Sun hat**

This is made of a 47-cm diameter circle of material, with an inner circle drawn on the wrong side 3 cm inside the edge for the casing. When drawing the round shapes for the sun hat, it helps if you can find a round bowl such as a mixing bowl, small washing-up bowl or washing-basket lid to draw round with tailor's chalk or pencil.
1 Turn and machine or hem a narrow, 0.75-cm wide, hem all round the hat edge.
2 Pin and tack bias binding round the casing circle as for the sun dress waist. Remove the pins and machine or hem along each edge.
3 Sew the lace trimming over the hem edge, the right side of the lace against the hem on the wrong side of the hat. Overlap the ends as for joining tape ends. Pin, tack, remove the pins and machine or hem the lace to the hat edge. Press the hat.
4 Thread elastic through the hat.

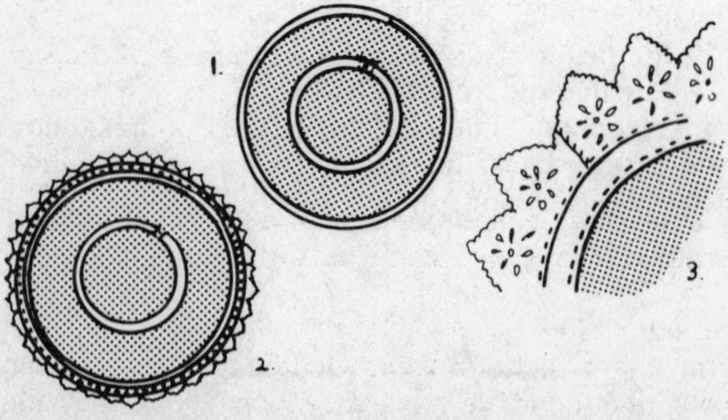


*1 narrow hem, pin and tack bias binding for casing 2 sew trimming over hem edge 3 close-up of trimming*

## *Elephant bib*

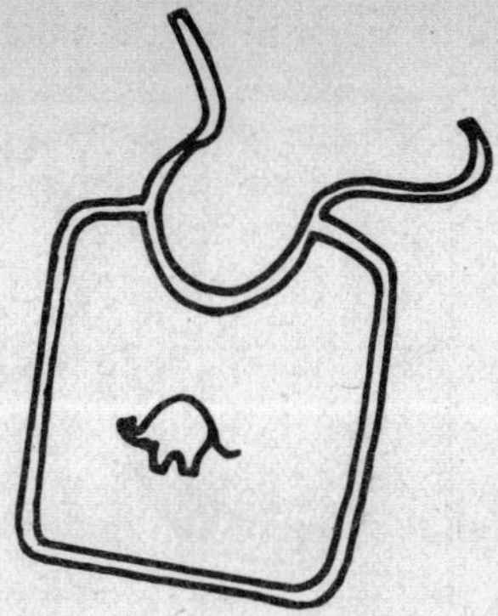

This bib is made of stretch towelling with a little red elephant stitched on the front, and is edged with red bias binding, with red binding tie strings. Sewing on a shape like the elephant is called appliqué.

**You will need**

30 cm long × 25 cm wide white stretch towelling
30 cm long × 25 cm wide white plastic material for lining
12 cm × 12 cm washable material for the elephant appliqué (not synthetic)
10 cm × 10 cm iron-on lightweight interfacing
2.3 metres bias binding
thread matching the bias binding
white thread

**Pattern**

Enlarge the bib pattern from the chart overleaf and cut out. Trace the elephant pattern, and the elephant's ear separately, from the page and cut out.

**To cut out**

Pin the bib pattern to the towelling and cut out one shape. Cut out one bib in plastic. Pin the elephant shape to the interfacing and cut out one shape. Remove the patterns and put away.

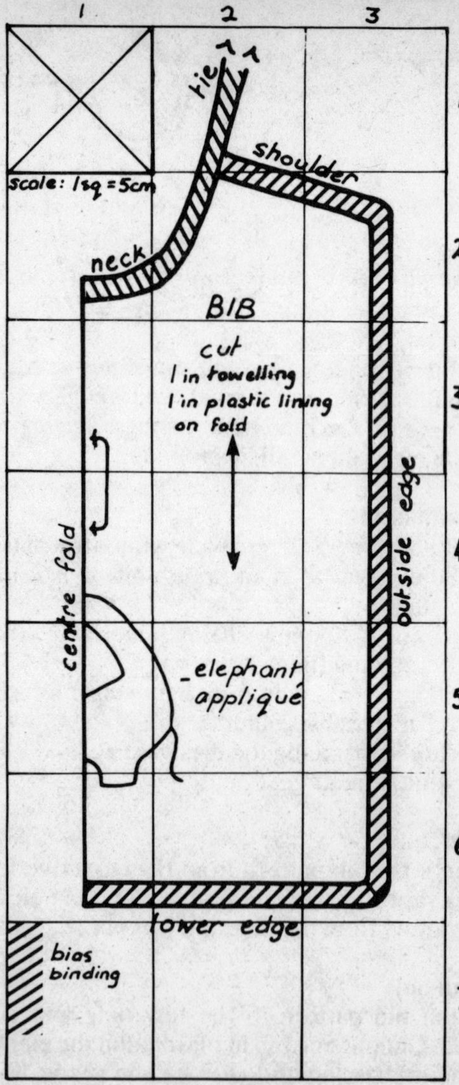

1
2
3
scale: 1sq = 5cm
tie
shoulder
neck
BIB
cut
1 in towelling
1 in plastic lining
on fold
centre fold
outside edge
elephant appliqué
lower edge
bias binding
1
2
3
4
5
6
7

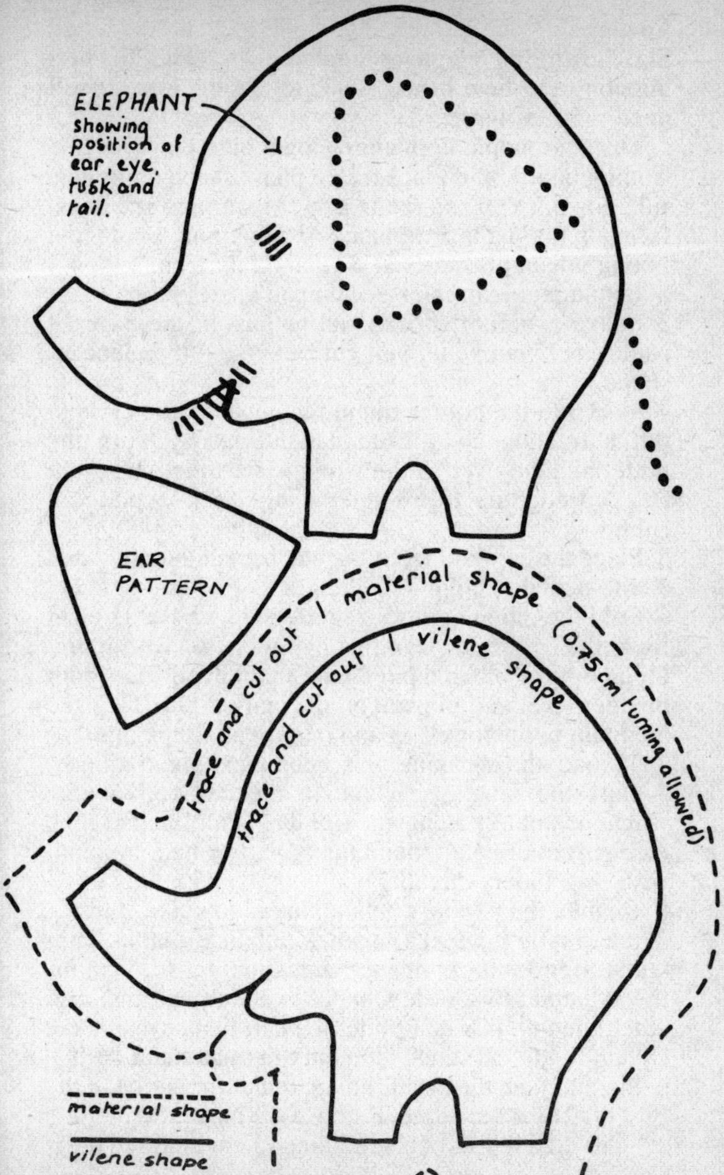
ELEPHANT
showing position of ear, eye, tusk and tail.
EAR PATTERN
trace and cut out 1 material shape (0.75cm turning allowed)
trace and cut out 1 vilene shape
material shape
vilene shape

**To make**

Start with the elephant appliqué and ask for permission, and help if necessary, to use the iron. It will need to be fairly hot.

1 Turn the appliqué material right side down on the ironing board, and place the elephant shape on it, glue side down. (You can see this by the shine on the interfacing.) Press the interfacing shape firmly on to the wrong side of the material. Switch off the iron.

2 Unplug the iron and stand it up in a safe place.

3 Leave a border of material to turn in the edge all round, 0.75 cm wide, and cut out round the elephant shape.

4 Snip into the border round the outside edge close to but a fraction away from the interfacing. Turn the material edge over to the wrong side, overlapping the snipped edge on to the interfacing. Tack in place all round.

5 Place the ear pattern on the elephant and draw round it with pencil or tailor's chalk.

6 Fold the bib in half from side to side, and mark 6 cm from the lower edge on this half-way fold with a pin. Open out the bib and pin the elephant in position, with his feet level and centred on the marker pin. Tack the elephant to the towelling and remove all the pins.

7 Thread the machine and bobbin with red thread. Adjust the sewing machine to medium-sized zigzag stitch, or small straight stitch, and carefully machine the elephant in place all round the edge. (Or hem by hand, with embroidery thread.)

8 Change the sewing machine thread to white, and the stitch to satin stitch at a narrow width, if available. Satin stitch round the ear shape. Satin stitch for 0.25 cm for the eye and sew a tusk. Change to red thread and satin stitch the tail. (Or embroider the ear, tusk, eye and tail by hand with backstitch, satin stitch or small chain stitch.)

9 Pin and tack the plastic lining to the wrong side of the bib, matching the edges. Remove the pins.

10 Cut off a length of bias binding 75 cm long and put it

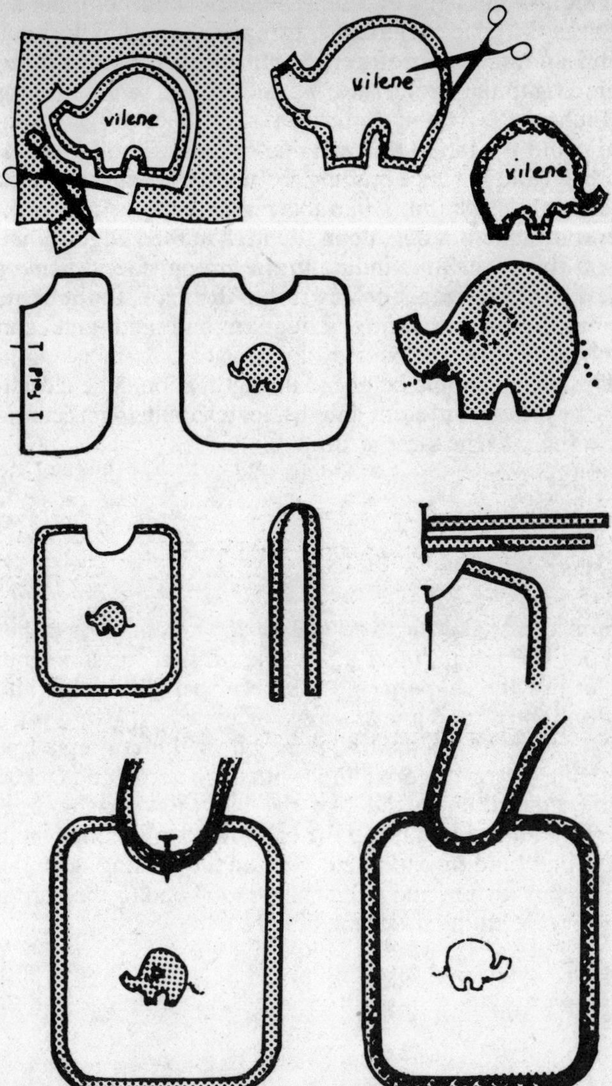
vilene
vilene
vilene

aside for the neck and tie strings. Sew bias binding all round the edge of the bib, starting at one side of the neck and ending at the other side. Instead of hemming the binding to the wrong side, if available you can use zigzag stitch.

11 Fold the bib in half and mark the centre of the neck edge. Fold the neck binding and mark the half-way mark along it with a pin. Align this pin with the centre neck, and sew the binding along the neck curved edge. When you turn over the binding to the wrong side to hem or sew it with zigzag stitching round the neck, at the same time fold the binding strings in half and tack and machine them (or oversew by hand) along their length. The strings should be of equal length, about 30 cm each. If they are of different lengths, match them together and cut them to the same size.

### *Oven square*

You can make an oven square for holding hot dishes from the bib pattern: a possible present for someone. Cut out the shape round the lower part of the bib and along the dotted line as shown on the chart, giving you a 20 cm × 20 cm square, rounded at the corners. Use strong cotton material lined with flannelette, and tacked together, then edged like the bib with bias binding. Leave an extra 16 cm at the end for a corner loop where the bias binding ends meet. Sew on the binding as for the bib, but turn in and oversew the loop end to the corner after machining it like the bib ties.

## *Strawberry pincushion*

If you're racking your brains for ideas for presents, this strawberry pincushion will be welcomed by anyone who sews. It could be useful for your own workbox too. You could also design your own pincushion following these instructions, such as a simple one made out of two felt circles, perhaps embroidered with some of the stitches described at the beginning of the book.

**You will need**

23-cm square of red felt
10-cm square of green felt
skein of bright green embroidery thread
kapok or similar fleecy stuffing

**Pattern**

Trace the pattern from the next page and cut out.

**To cut out**

Pin the pattern close to the edge of the folded red felt and cut out one strawberry shape. Cut out a second shape in the same way. Pin the leaf pattern to the green felt and cut out carefully. Embroidery scissors will be useful for cutting into the shape if you have got some.

Transfer the position of the french knot marker dots to the felt by sticking pins through the pattern on to one of the red felt shapes through the dots. Mark where the pins come through with tailor's chalk. Remove the pins and the pattern and put it away.

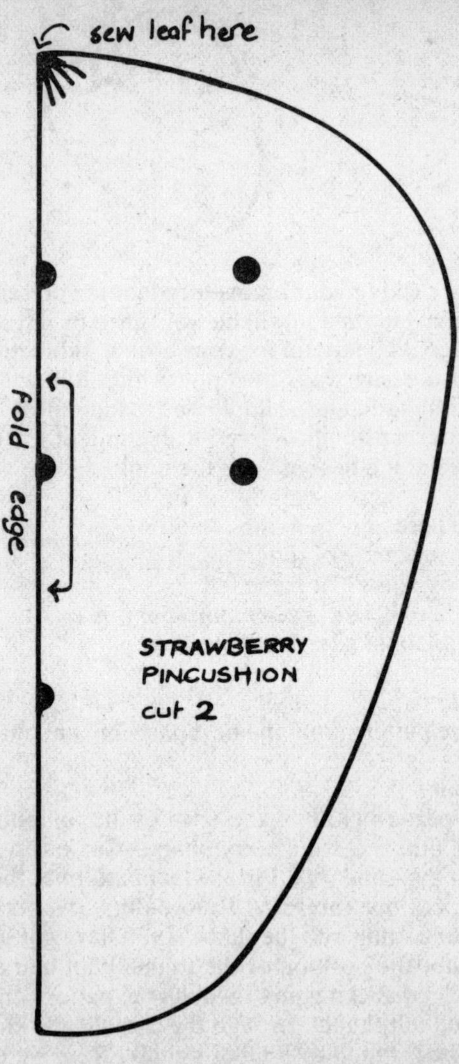
sew leaf here
fold edge
STRAWBERRY
PINCUSHION
cut 2

strawberry pincushion leaves
trace full size and cut out
one in green felt.

**To make**

1 Embroider the french knots with the green thread. (See page 29.) These knots represent the strawberry seeds on the skin.

2 Place the two red felt shapes together and pin and tack them round the edge. Remove the pins. Using green embroidery thread, oversew the shapes together all round the edge except for the opening for the stuffing.

3 Push kapok into the opening in the side of the pincushion right into all the parts of the strawberry shape, until the strawberry is firmly, but not over, stuffed. Oversew the gap to close the sides.

4 Re-thread the needle with green embroidery thread, and secure the thread to the broad top of the strawberry with one or two small backstitches. Pass the needle

through from under the centre of the leaf shape and draw the thread through, so the leaf is held against the strawberry. Keep it in place, and sew it to the strawberry with two or three small backstitches at the centre. Take the needle through the strawberry and snip off the thread close to the surface.

## *Dolls' clothes*

From these patterns for dolls' clothes you can make a complete wardrobe for your doll, and use the patterns to design some for yourself. There's a plain dress with sleeves, from which you can make a petticoat, a T-shirt, a pyjama top, a skirt and a school tunic; and there's a pair of trousers for pants, pyjama trousers and jeans. The bunchy best dress could be used for a long baby gown too, and the felt coat and hood can convert to a jacket and separate bonnet. How to make different sizes is given with the patterns. Use oddments of material for the clothes if you can.

*Key to pattern opposite*

A doll's dress, T shirt and petticoat
B sleeve for A
CD short pants and long trousers
E puff sleeve for F
F party dress

1 cm seams allowed

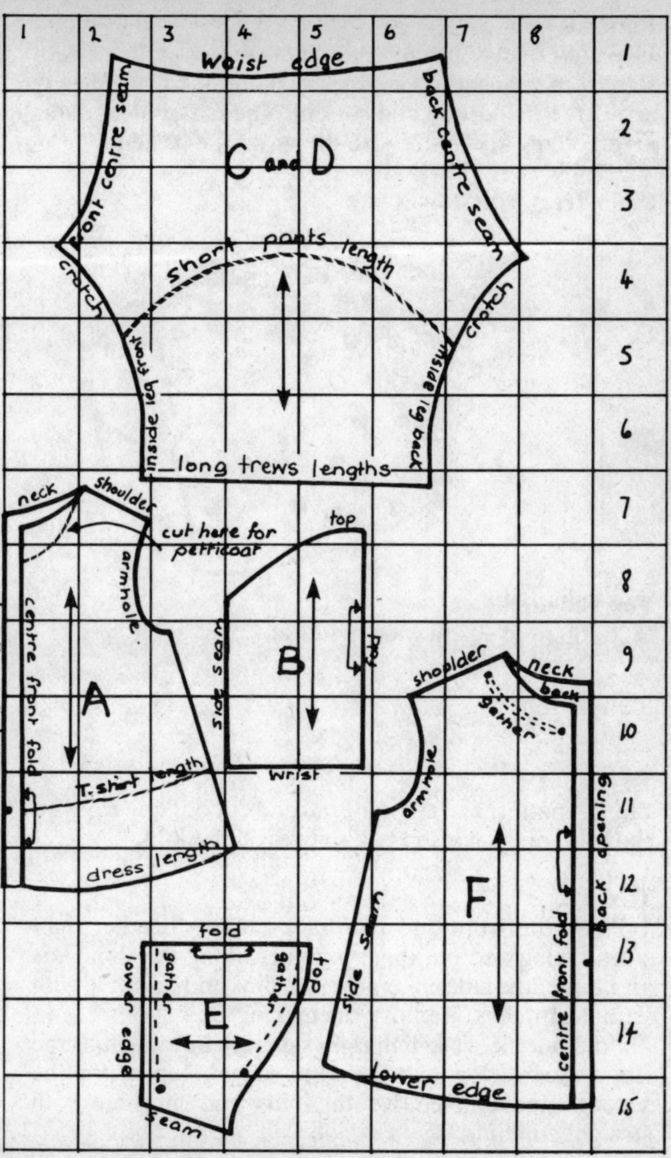

1
2
3
4
5
6
7
8
waist edge
front centre seam
back centre seam
C and D
short pants length
crotch
crotch
inside leg front
inside leg back
long trews lengths
neck
shoulder
cut here for petticoat
armhole
back opening
centre front fold
A
T. shirt length
dress length
top
side seam
B
fold
wrist
shoulder
neck
back
gather
armhole
F
back opening
centre front fold
side seam
lower edge
fold
lower edge
gather
gather
top
E
seam
9
10
11
12
13
14
15

**Patterns**
Use your own doll's measurements to adjust the pattern size from the charts. Enlarge the patterns to include any adjustments needed and cut out. The material amounts given below are for the size shown on the pattern.

**Plain dress with sleeves**

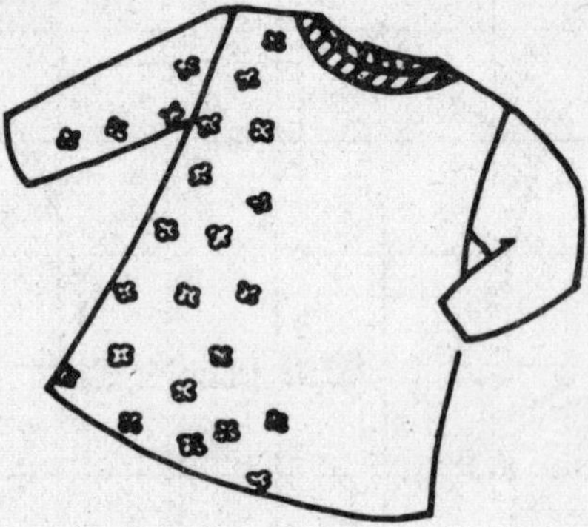

**You will need**

30 cm of 90-cm wide material
3 small buttons
20 cm bias binding
thread

**To cut out**
Pin the patterns to the material and cut out one front on the fold; one back and two sleeves on the fold.

**To make**
1 Place the front and two back shapes together right sides facing and pin them together along the shoulders and down the sides. Remove the pins and machine with straight stitches. Remove the tacking.
2 Fold one sleeve in half right sides facing, matching the sleeve seam. Pin and tack the seam. Repeat for the second sleeve. Remove the pins and machine with straight stitching.

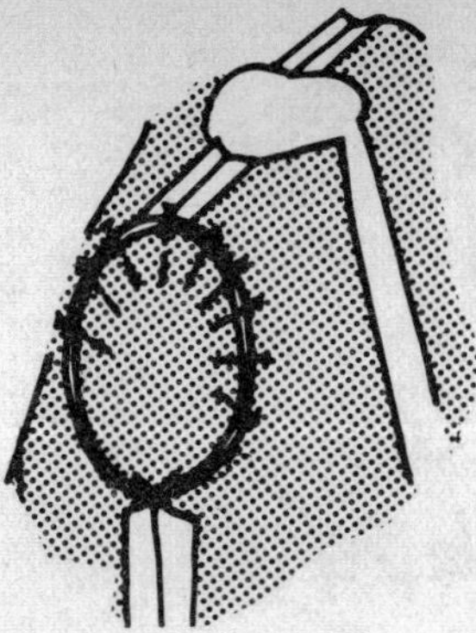

3 Open the armhole, and with right sides facing, fit the top of the sleeve into it, matching the sleeve seam and dress side seams. Pin the top of the sleeve and armhole together all round, then tack. Do the same with the second sleeve and armhole. Remove the pins and machine all round where tacked, then remove the tacking.
4 Sew 1-cm hems down each side of the dress back opening, and machine or hem.
5 Turn, and hem or machine 1-cm wide hems round the sleeves and the dress hem.
6 Sew bias binding along the neck edge.
7 *Buttons and buttonholes*
(a) Mark the position of the three buttons on the left-hand hem down the back opening: the first, 0.75 cm below the bias binding; the second, 6 cm below that, and the third, 6 cm below the second. Sew a button on at each mark. (See page 39 for sewing on buttons.)
(b) Buttonholes: on the right-hand hem down the back opening, mark three buttonholes to correspond with the buttons. Sew the buttonholes as expained on page 40, using the blanket stitch version.
8 Press the dress.

## Pyjamas

**You will need**

50 cm of 90-cm wide nursery flannelette
20 cm bias binding
3 small press fasteners
40 cm narrow elastic
thread

**To cut out**

Pin on the patterns and cut out one front on the fold and two backs, two sleeves and two trouser shapes.

**To make the top**

Follow the instructions for making the day dress, but instead of buttons and buttonholes, sew on press fasteners. For details of how to do this see page 42.

**To make the trousers**

1 With right sides facing place the two trouser shapes together and pin and tack down the centre front seam and centre back seam. Remove the pins and machine with straight stitches. Remove the tacking.

2 Rearrange the trousers so that, right sides facing, the seams lie down the centre front and centre back. Pin and tack together down the inside leg seams at each side.

Remove the pins, and machine the seams. Remove the tacking.

3 Turn and pin a 1-cm hem round the waist, and round each leg end. Tack and remove the pins, then machine the hems, leaving a 2-cm opening in the waist hem for threading the elastic through.

4 Press the pyjamas.

5 Thread the elastic through the waist hem of the trousers as shown on page 48, and trim and join the elastic ends. Oversew the opening.

**Pants and petticoat**

**You will need**

40 cm of white cotton lawn 90 cm wide
1.2 metres broderie anglaise trimming 2 cm wide, or lace trimming if wished
40 cm narrow elastic
2 small press fasteners
thread

**To cut out**

Pin the patterns to the material and cut out two pants' shapes; one petticoat front on the fold, and one petticoat back on the fold.

**To make the pants**

1 Pin, tack, remove the pins and machine as for the pyjama trousers centre front and inside leg seams.
2 Turn and pin a narrow hem, 0.75 cm wide, round each pants' leg. Tack, remove the pins, then machine. Remove the tacking.
3 Turn and machine a 1-cm wide hem round the pants' waist, leaving an opening for the elastic.
4 Trim the irregularly-shaped top edge of the broderie anglaise trimming level all along. Turn this edge over on to the right side 0.25 cm, and place this turned-over edge, right side against the hem, on the wrong side of the pants' leg, and pin close to the edge. Pin broderie anglaise all round the hem, and at the end, with 1.5 cm

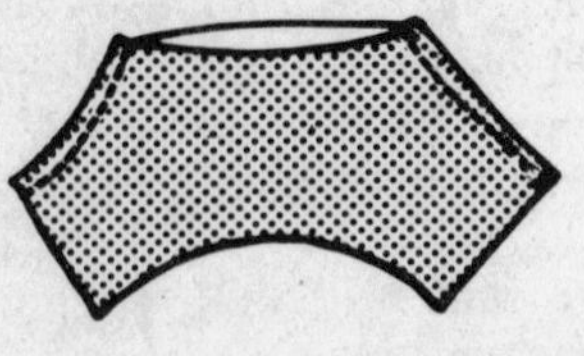

allowed for the overlap and join, cut off any surplus. Trim the other pants' leg in the same way.

5 Turn in the ends of the broderie anglaise to overlap and join them as for tape (see page 48). Tack the trimming in place round both pants' legs and remove the pins.

6 Machine close to the top edge of the trimming, and across the join. Remove the tacking and press the pants.

7 Thread elastic through the waist hem, and draw up to fit. Trim and join the ends then oversew the opening.

**To make the petticoat**

1 Place the petticoat front and back right sides together, and join the side seams, and the right-hand shoulder seam (which seems like the left-hand one when the material is wrong side out) as for the plain dress.

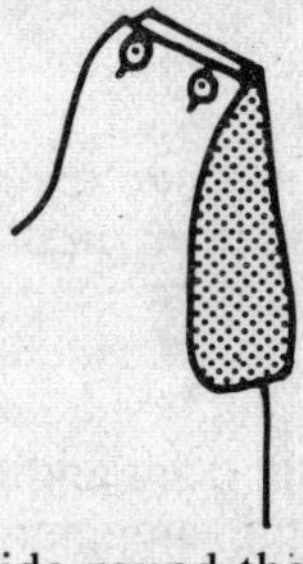

2 Turn narrow hems 0.5 cm wide round the petticoat neck, armholes, and lower edge. Pin and tack, and remove the pins. Turn 0.75-cm hems along the front and back open shoulder edge. Machine all round the neck edge across the shoulder, round the left-hand armhole and along the other shoulder. Machine the right-hand armhole hem, and the lower edge hem.

3 Attach broderie anglaise trimming round the petticoat lower edge hem as for the pants' legs.

4 Overlap the open shoulder front hem on to the back hem. Sew a small press fastener at each end of the overlapped hems, to fasten them.

5 Press the petticoat.

**Best dress**

**You will need**

40 cm of 90-cm wide material
80 cm bias binding
30 cm narrow velvet ribbon
3 small buttons
thread

**To cut out**

Pin the pattern to the material, folded as required, and cut out one front on the fold, two necks and two sleeves on the fold.

**To make**

1 Place the front and back shapes right sides together, and join the shoulder and side seams as for the plain dress. Fold the sleeves in half, matching the edges, and join the seams as for the plain dress sleeves. Hem the sides of the back opening.
2 Sew bias binding along the neck edge and round the sleeve ends.
3 Sew in the sleeves. To gather the top of the sleeves to fit the armholes, sew a row of gathering stitches between the marks for gathering at the top of the sleeve.
4 Draw up the gathering thread at the top of one sleeve, with the material turned right side out, so the sleeve fits inside the armhole. Anchor the thread end round a pin. Pin the sleeve into the armhole as for the plain dress and adjust the gathers to fit exactly. Tack all round. Fit and

pin the other sleeve in the second armhole the same way. Remove the pins and machine the sleeves into the armholes. Remove the tacking and gathering threads.

5 Turn up a 1-cm hem all round the dress lower edge and hem or machine.

6 Sew three buttonholes and buttons down the back of the dress to fasten the opening, as for the plain dress.

7 Gather the neck and sleeves 1.5 cm from the edge to fit the neck and arms of the doll – in the case of our pattern to 16 cm for the neck and 14 cm circumference

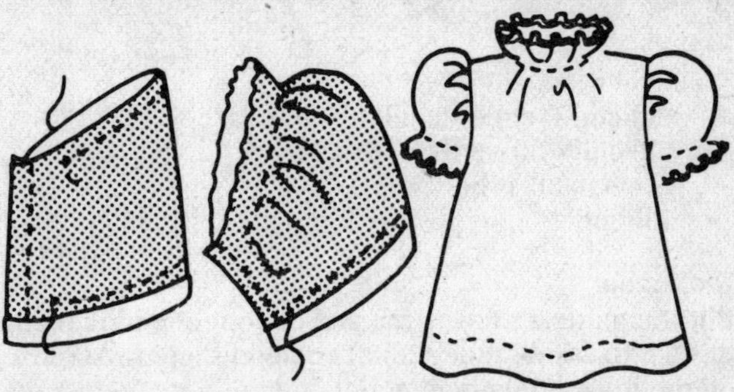

for the arm. Secure the gathering threads and trim, then machine over the gathering rows with straight stitches. This is called 'shirring', and rows of gathering like this can be made by hand or machine.

8 Slipstitch a band of velvet ribbon over the neck-edge shirring, and make a small bow with the rest of the velvet ribbon and sew it on the front.

9 Press the dress.

**Gathers**

Gathering is done with similar stitches to running stitch or tacking stitch, though with slightly longer stitches, usually about 0.75 cm long, and smaller spaces, about 0.25 cm. Start at the right, with a knotted long thread, and sew along the row to be gathered. Leave a long thread end unsecured, but wind it round a pin in a figure of eight to anchor it. Draw up the thread to gather.

**Coat**

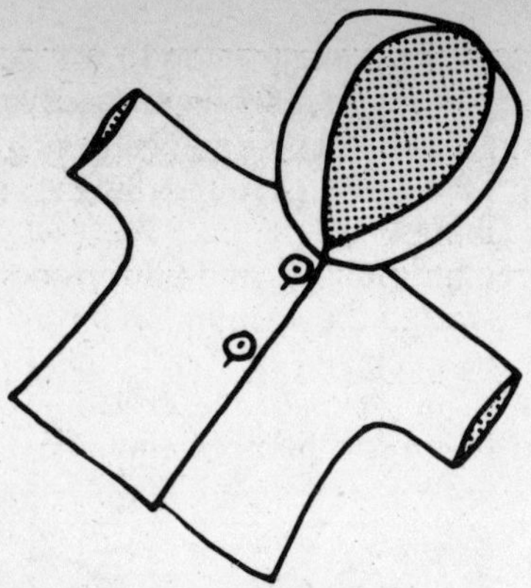

**You will need**

30 cm 90-cm wide felt for the coat
25 cm × 50 cm felt for the hood
2 small brass buttons
thread

**To cut out**

Pin the patterns to the felt and cut out one back on the fold, two front shapes, and two hood shapes. Allow for hems as for ordinary material.

**To make**

1 Place the coat fronts over the coat backs, with right sides facing (though felt is reversible, your material might not be). Pin together along the shoulder from the neck to the wrist edge, and from the wrist edge underarm down the side seam to the lower coat edge. Do the same for the other side. Tack where pinned and remove the pins, then machine.
2 Place the hood sides together right sides facing, and pin and tack from the top front to the back lower edge. Remove the pins and machine.
3 Open out the coat, right side out, and open out the hood. Place the hood lower edge against the coat neck edge right sides facing, and pin and tack them together all along. Remove the pins and machine. Remove the tacking.

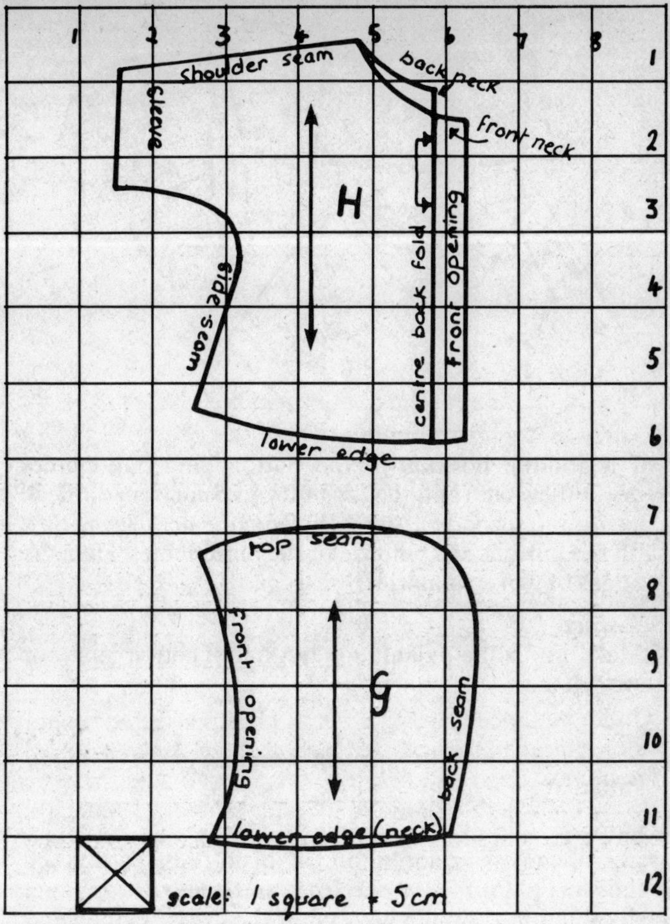


G 'hood' and Coat hood
H coat

1 cm seams allowed

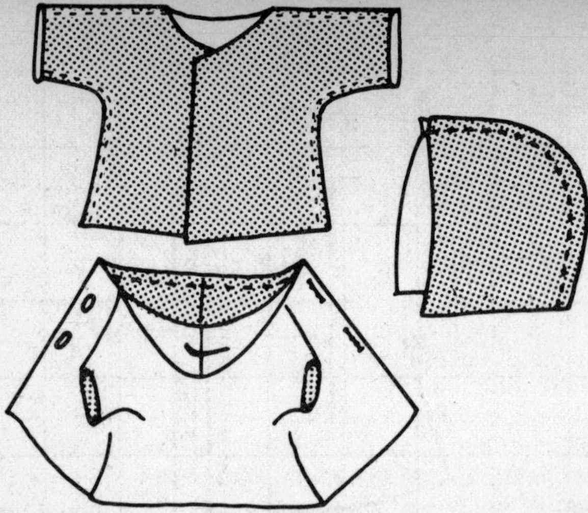

4 Mark the position of the buttons and buttonholes down the coat front, the top button 1.5 cm from the neck seam, the second button 9 cm from the neck seam. Sew on the buttons and embroider the buttonholes. Hem the edges of woven material. Press.

**T-shirt**
Make as for the pyjama top but out of cotton jersey or stretch terry.

**Jeans**
Make the pyjama trousers in denim, and sew with red stitching.

**Skirt**
Cut off below armholes on the plain dress pattern for the skirt pattern. Cut one front and one back, join the sides and turn up the hem as for the dress. Turn over a 1-cm wide hem round the waist, and thread with elastic.

**Long dresses, short jackets**
Lengthen or shorten the patterns along the lines where indicated.

**Hood as bonnet**
Gather the neck edge and sew ties at the front corners.

## *Sports gear*

With the vest, shorts and track suit patterns given here, plus the duffel bag on page 129, you can make yourself a complete kit for sports events, jogging, cross-country running or school sports days.

The vest and shorts are made out of medium-weight nylon jersey, and the track suit out of fleecy lined heavy cotton jersey material, both of them decorated with braid bands, an optional addition.

These fabrics are usually sold in wider widths, 115 cm or 140 cm, which gives you more leeway for cutting out. With larger items like this it really is worthwhile looking for the material at the sales. It could be a big saving.

Before you begin to make these items, it would be as well to remind yourself of the advice on sewing knits, given on page 16. To recap, because the stretch fabric may be pulled in wear, the stitchline could break. This is why it is best to use strong thread, and stretch or small zigzag stitches on the machine, if available, or small straight stitch with a second row beside the first (as insurance). In these patterns 2-cm wide seams have been allowed to take account of the knit fabric.

### Vest and shorts

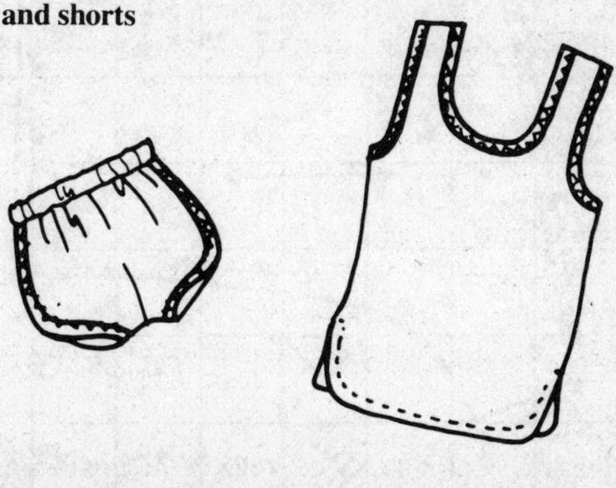

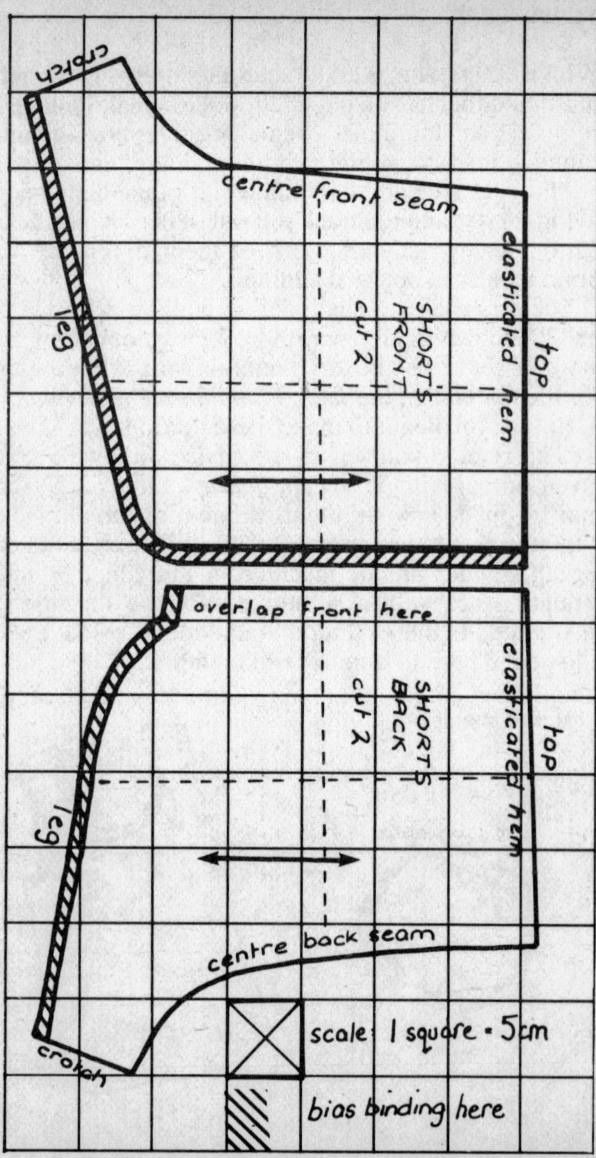

crotch
centre front seam
top
elasticated hem
SHORTS FRONT
cut 2
leg
overlap front here
top
elasticated hem
SHORTS BACK
cut 2
leg
centre back seam
crotch
scale: 1 square = 5cm
bias binding here

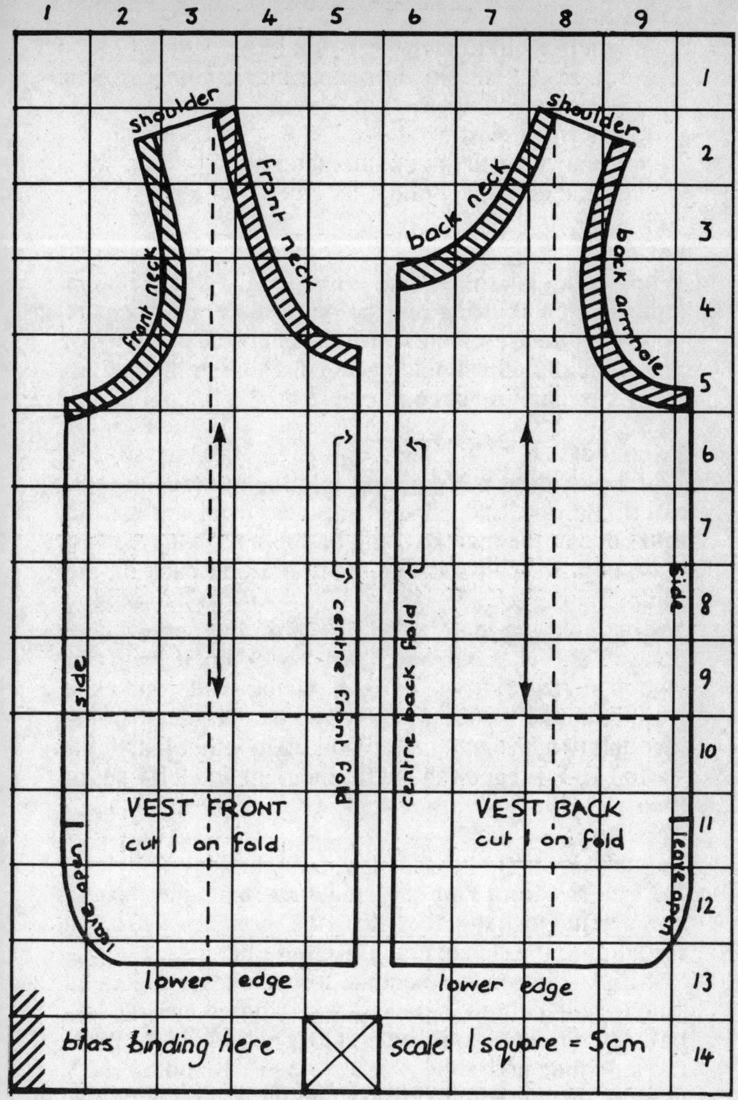

1 2 3 4 5 6 7 8 9
1 2 3 4 5 6 7 8 9 10 11 12 13 14
shoulder
front neck
front neck
side
centre front fold
VEST FRONT
cut 1 on fold
leave open
lower edge
shoulder
back neck
back armhole
side
centre back fold
VEST BACK
cut 1 on fold
leave open
lower edge
bias binding here
scale: 1 square = 5cm

**You will need**

- 2 metres of 115-cm wide nylon jersey
- 4.6 metres of folded braid or bias binding, 2.5 cm wide when opened out
- 1 metre of elastic
- thread to match track suit material
- thread to match braid

**Pattern**

When enlarged, the pattern is for size 12 (girls'). Before enlarging and cutting out the pattern shapes, compare your own measurements with the chart measurements, and plan any adjustments needed. Enlarge the pattern from the chart and cut out.

**To cut out**

*Vest* Follow the pattern, and fold the material as indicated. Pin the fold edge of the vest front against the fold edge of the material, and do the same with the vest back pattern. Cut out one front and one back on the fold.

*Shorts* Fold the material as shown on the pattern, and pin the shorts' front and shorts' back on it over two layers of material wrong sides facing. Cut round the front and back patterns to give you two of each. Cutting through two layers of material faced together like this is so that you will get a shape for the right and left sides of the shorts, both right sides out, when made up.

**To make the vest**

1 Place the front and back together right sides facing, and pin and tack together along the shoulders and down the sides to the side opening. Remove the pins.

Adjust the sewing machine to one of the suggested stitches for knitted material. A sharp new needle or a ball-point needle would be best to use, if available. Place the stitchline under the needle, and slowly and carefully guiding the material to avoid rumpling or stretching it as it is stitched, machine the shoulder and side seams. Sew a second row of machine stitches for straight stitch, parallel and very close to the first.

2 Adjust the machine to medium-sized zigzag stitch for the hems, or stay with the present stitch. Wrong side out, turn up a 1.5-cm hem along the lower edge, which curves up at the sides towards the seams. Pin and tack the hem, front and back, using a lot of tacking stitches to keep the rather slippery nylon knit material in place. Remove the pins, and slowly machine along the hem. If you are using a zigzag stitch take the stitches just across the hem edge. If machining with straight stitches, put the second row of stitching 0.75 cm above the first.

3 Change over to white thread on the bobbin and needle, to match the braid. Allow 3 cm spare to begin with, as braid is inclined to fray. Place the braid over the neck edge, with the wide side inside, and pin through all three layers, keeping the vest edge into the fold of the braid. Keep the braid smooth and even over the vest edge, and continue pinning it all round. At the end, trim the braid end to 2 cm; trim the other end and turn in and overlap the braid end on to it. Pin. Tack all round and remove the pins, then machine.

4 Sew braid all round the armholes by the same method.

**To make the shorts**

1 Place the front shapes together right sides facing, and pin and tack the centre seam. Repeat for the back shapes.

2 Adjust the machine to the seam stitch chosen, and thread to match the nylon jersey. Remove the pins and machine the centre front and back seams. Remove the tacking.

3 Right sides facing, place the shorts front and back over each other, and pin and tack together along the crotch seam. Remove the pins and machine.

4 Open out the shorts and pin and tack braid along the front side edges, from the front waist to the leg edge, then on round the legs, to the lower end of the side seams at the back. Change to white thread on the machine and

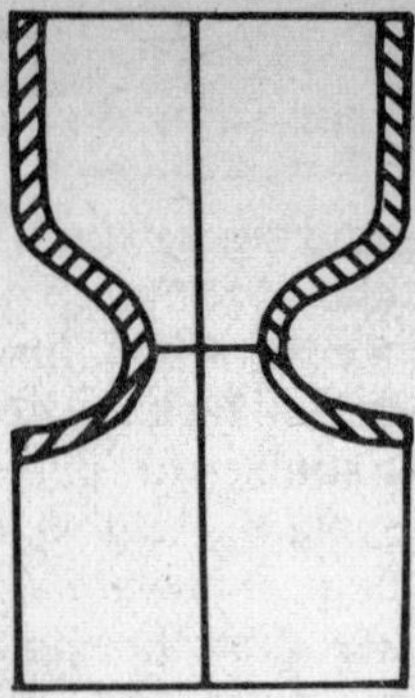

straight stitches. Machine the braid in place as on the vest.

5 Right sides out, fold the shorts front and back up to match the side seams and waist edges. Overlap the braid edge over the seam allowance of the back edge down the side and pin together down both sides. Tack this overlapped seam to join the front to the back.

6 Machine the braid edge on to the shorts back, close to the edge, from the right side.

7 Change back to thread matching the main material, and the seam stitch you have been using, on the sewing machine. Turn the waist edge over for a 1.5-cm wide hem, on the wrong side, and pin and tack. Remove the pins and machine, leaving a 2-cm opening for threading through the elastic. Remove the tacking.

8 Thread elastic through the hem, trim to size and join the ends. Oversew the opening in the hem.

**Track suit**

**You will need**

3.5 metres of 115-cm wide material
4 metres of 2.5-cm wide braid
3.5 metres of elastic
1 metre of cord
thread to match track suit and braid
5 cm bias binding for ends of cord

**Pattern**

The chart is drawn to size 12 (Girls'). Check the measurements of the track suit pattern against your own measurements and alter where required. Enlarge the pattern from the chart, taking the alterations, if any, into account. Cut out the pattern shapes.

**To cut out**

Refer to the patterns on pages 114 and 115 for folding the material and pinning on the patterns. Cut out one back and one front for the top, on the fold. For the sleeve shapes, pin the pattern to two layers of material wrong sides together, to get reverse shapes for the left and right arm. The same applies to the trousers, for the right and left sides.

**To make**

If using braid, it is best to sew it on first. Adjust the sewing machine to straight stitches, and thread it to match the braid. Mark the position of the braid on the right side of the material.

1 Fold the first sleeve in half from side to side, matching the sleeve seam edges. Mark down the fold with pins, then open out the sleeve. Place a ruler beside the pins and mark beside the pins with tailor's chalk. Remove the pins and complete the chalk line.

2 With the sleeve flat on the table, right side uppermost, start at the centre top and pin braid over the chalk line

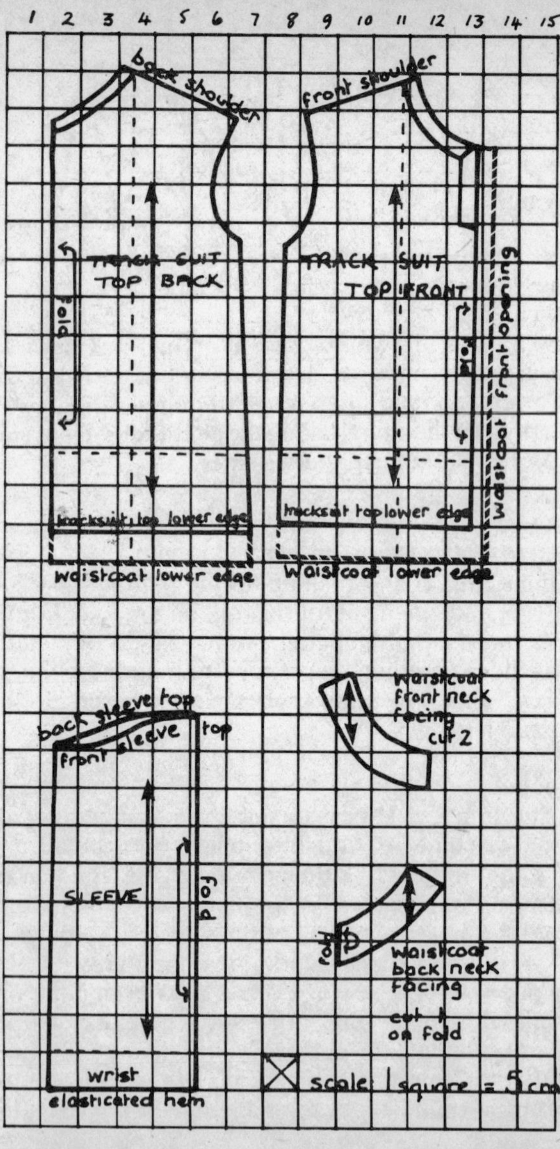

1 2 3 4 5 6 7 8 9 10 11 12 13 14 15
back shoulder
front shoulder
TRACK SUIT TOP BACK
TRACK SUIT TOP FRONT
fold
fold
front opening
waistcoat
tracksuit top lower edge
tracksuit top lower edge
waistcoat lower edge
waistcoat lower edge
waistcoat front neck facing cut 2
back sleeve top
front sleeve top
SLEEVE
fold
wrist
elasticated hem
fold
waistcoat back neck facing
cut 1 on fold
scale: 1 square = 5 cm

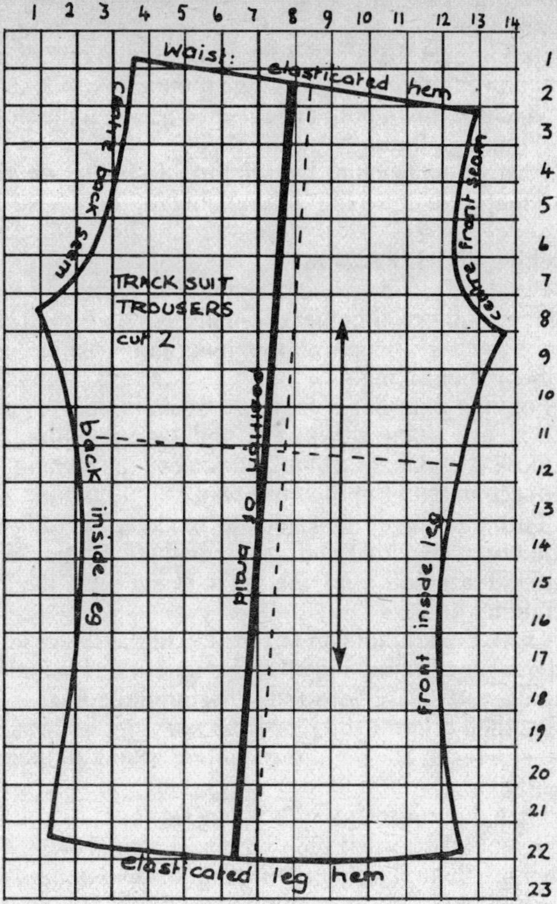


scale: 1 square = 5 cm

from top to wrist, so the chalk line is under the centre of the braid. Tack the braid in place along both edges and remove the pins. Be careful to keep the braid and the material level together. Tack braid on the other sleeve and down the trouser legs in the same way.

3 Machine down both edges of the braid on the sleeves and the legs. Press.

4 Change the machine over to thread to match the track suit material, and to a stitch suitable for the seams.

**Making the track suit top**

1 Place the top front and back together right sides facing and pin and tack together down the side seams and along the shoulders. Remove the pins and machine, then remove the tacking.

2 Fold the right-hand sleeve from side to side, matching the sleeve seam edges. Pin and tack together, then remove the pins. Machine and remove the tacking. Sew the second sleeve in the same way.

3 Turn the sleeves right side out, but keep the top wrong side out. Check that you are pinning the left sleeve into the left armhole and the right sleeve into the right armhole.

Open the armhole and fit the top of the sleeve into it, aligning the seams. Pin all round and tack. Pin and tack the second sleeve into the other armhole in the same way, then remove the pins from both sleeves. Machine the sleeves in all round the armhole seams and remove the tacking.

4 Turn the top and sleeves wrong side out. Turn 1.5-cm hems round the waist and sleeve edges, and pin, tack and machine them. Use zigzag stitches or the seam stitch as before, and leave an opening in each hem for threading through the elastic.

5 Pin and tack folded braid over the neck edge, starting from one shoulder seam, as for sewing braid on the vest and shorts. Where the braid turns for the front opening at the corner, mitre it with a pleat. Make a similar mitre at the lowest point of the front opening, and at the other

corner by the neck. When braid has been tacked all round the neck, and the ends trimmed, turned in and overlapped as for the vest, before machining, oversew the mitred pleats in place by hand. Remove all pins. Change the machine to thread matching the braid, and to straight stitching. Machine the braid to the neck edge close to the braid edge.
6 Thread elastic through the sleeve and waist hems, and trim and join the ends. Oversew the openings in the hems.

7 Cut two lengths of cord, each 30 cm, and oversew inside each corner of the top front opening with tape on top. Knot the cord ends to prevent fraying.

**Making the track suit trousers**
1 Sew on the braid in the same way as you did for the top, where shown on the pattern.
2 Place the shapes together right sides facing, and pin together down the centre front and centre back seams. Tack and remove the pins. Put thread matching the track suit material on the machine, and adjust if necessary to the seam stitch being used. Machine the tacked seams, then remove the tacking.
3 With the right sides facing, place the front over the back of the trousers and match the inside leg seams. Pin together down each side from the crotch to the leg end. Tack and remove the pins, and machine. Remove the tacking.
4 Turn 1.5-cm wide hems round the trousers' waist edge and round the leg ends. Sew the hems with an opening

for the elastic as for the track suit top.
5 Thread elastic through the waist and leg hems, and oversew the hem openings.

## *Wall tidy*

You can keep your homework or socks or hair ribbons in a wall tidy like this, and not only help to improve the looks of your room, but help you to always know where to find these things.

**You will need**

a furnishing material remnant 60 cm long × 120 cm wide
butterfly appliqué 15 cm × 10 cm felt per butterfly
1.5 metres bias binding 2.5 cm wide
thread
60 cm of wood dowelling 1.5 cm in diameter

**Pattern**
Enlarge the pattern shapes from the chart and cut out. Trace and cut out the butterfly pattern from page 68, or the elephant pattern on page 87. Transfer the pattern marks on to the right side of the fabric.

**To cut out**
Cut out one back and two pockets in the material, and as many butterflies or elephants as you like.

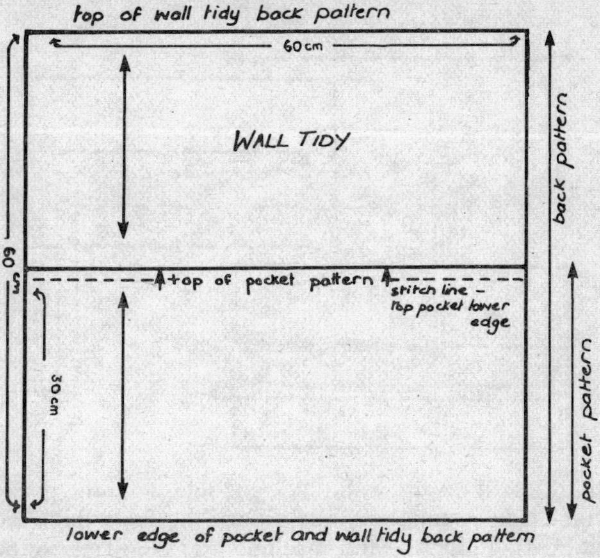


**To make**

1 Pockets: turn and machine 2-cm wide hems along the top edge of each pocket.
2 Butterflies: pin the butterflies (or elephants) on the pockets where you wish, but not across the seam allowance anywhere. Sew on round the edge. (See elephant appliqué, page 88, for details of how to do this.)
3 Turn the wall tidy back wrong side uppermost, and place the lower pocket right side over it, matching the lower edge. Machine together along the lower edge, for a 1.5-cm seam. Remove the tacking and turn the pocket up on the right side. Pin to the wall tidy right side down each side.
4 Match the lower edge of the second pocket against the

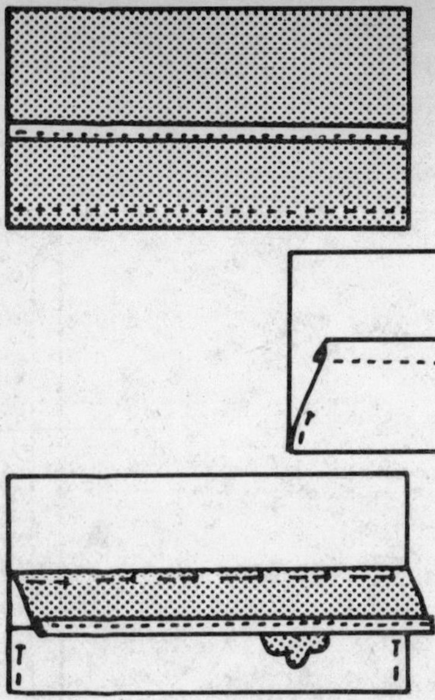

mark for it on the wall tidy right side, with the pocket right side against the tidy (it will lie over the lower pocket). Pin, tack and machine across just above the lower pocket for a 1.5-cm seam. Remove the tacking and turn the pocket up and pin to the tidy sides, like the lower pocket.

5 Tack the sides of the pockets to the tidy from top to bottom, remove the pins and machine down each side, 1 cm from the edge. Remove the tacking.

6 Sew bias binding down each side to cover the raw edges, over both pockets and tidy.

7 Divide the pockets into smaller pockets to suit the size of the items to go in them. Rule lines for the divisions down them with tailor's chalk, then machine straight stitches over these lines.

8 Turn and machine a 2-cm wide hem along the top edge. Slip the dowelling through this hem, and hang up the wall tidy with a tape loop tied to each end and hung on picture hooks.

## *Cat toy*

This cat toy is easy to make, and could be sewn from dressmaking oddments. It would make an ideal present. And there's a felt mouse to go with it you could make afterwards. Have a large knitting needle handy to help with the stuffing.

**You will need**

needlecord, jersey, cotton or a thin wool oddment 40 cm long × 50 cm wide
kapok
scraps of pink turquoise and black felt for eyes and nose
pink embroidery thread for mouth
white thread for whiskers
thread to match the material
60 cm of 2-cm wide velvet ribbon
glue suitable for sticking material

**Pattern**

Enlarge the pattern from the chart and cut out. Trace the features from the page separately and cut out.

**To cut out**

Fold the material wrong sides facing and pin on the cat pattern. Cut through two layers for shapes so you end up with reverse shapes. Cut out two blue eyes, two black pupils and one pink nose from the felt.

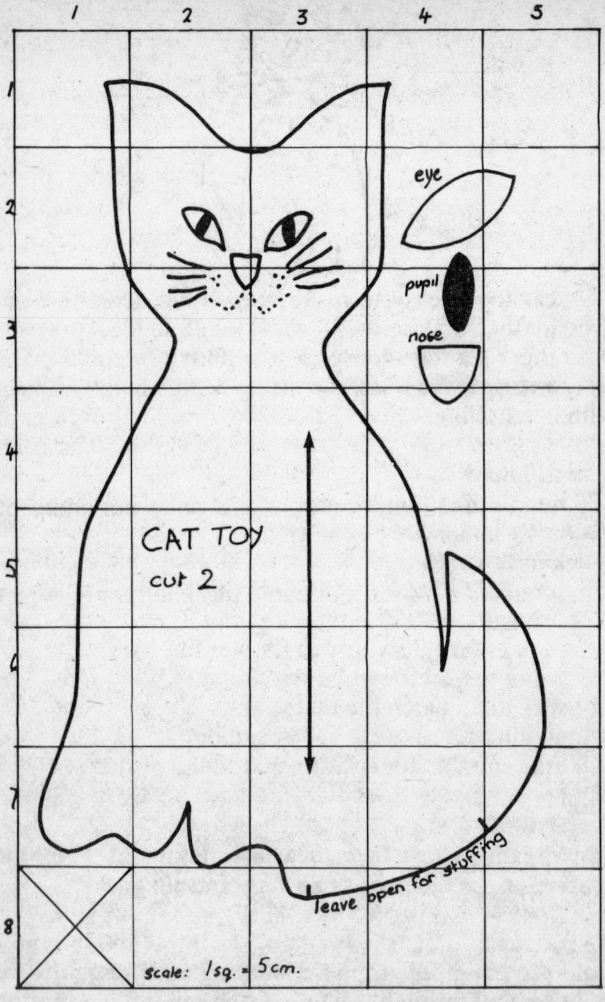
1
2
3
4
5
1
2
3
4
5
6
7
8
eye
pupil
nose
CAT TOY
cut 2
leave open for stuffing
scale: 1sq. = 5cm.

**To make**

1 Place the cat shapes together right sides facing, matching the edges all round, and pin. Tack together round the edges and remove the pins, except for the opening for the stuffing.

2 Adjust the machine for straight stitching. Machine the cat shapes together except along the stuffing opening, with a 1-cm wide seam. Remove the tacking. Snip into the seam allowance where shown but not through the stitches, and turn the cat right side out.

3 Stuff the cat through the opening, and use the blunt end of a knitting needle to help you push the kapok right into the points of the ears and tail. The cat should be firmly stuffed but fairly flat. When filled, turn in and oversew the sides of the stuffing opening together.

4 Embroider the cat's mouth with backstitch taken up and down as shown, with pink embroidery thread.

5 Glue on the features. Hold each felt shape on a pin and dab some glue on the back. Press it on the face. Glue the black felt pupils on top of the blue eyes.

6 Sew on white thread whiskers. Thread a needle with white thread but do not knot the thread end. Make a small backstitch in the face between the mouth and nose, leaving at tail about 5 cm long. Hold the thread down with your thumb so it doesn't pull out. Make a second pair of whiskers close beside the first, then two more pairs on the other side of the nose. Trim to 4 cm long when finished.

7 Tie a velvet ribbon bow at the back of the cat's neck. If the cat is a present for a baby, stitch a ribbon collar on instead.

## *Mouse*

It will be fun and no effort to make this felt mouse. You can choose other colours than the ones I suggest. If you make it out of woven material, remember to allow 1-cm seams.

**You will need**

donkey grey or beige felt 23 cm square
small pieces of brown felt for the ears and black and white felt for the eyes
coloured embroidery thread for sewing the mouse, plus pink or black for the mouse's nose, and white thread for the whiskers
kapok or cotton-wool stuffing
glue

**Pattern**

Trace the pattern from the page and cut out.

**To cut out**

Cut out two felt sides, one underside in main colour felt, two brown ears, two white eyes and two black pupils.

**To make**

1 Place the mouse sides together, matching the shapes, and using coloured embroidery thread oversew from the tip of the nose to the tail.
2 Open out the mouse sides and pin the base to the lower edges of the sides. Tack, leaving about 3 cm open for stuffing. Remove the pins and oversew with embroidery thread.
3 Stuff the mouse firmly, right up into the nose, and put plenty of stuffing in to give him a good humped back.

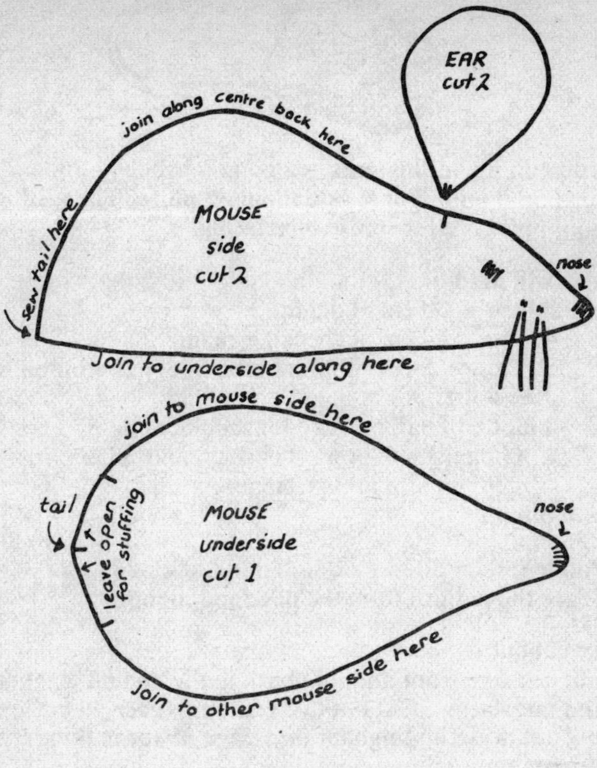


When stuffed, pull the sides of the opening together and oversew them with embroidery thread. Take the needle out at the tail end and cut off the thread leaving a 10-cm long tail. Knot the end if you are using stranded embroidery thread.

4 Oversew the ears on top of the head.

5 Satin stitch the nose with black embroidery thread.

6 Using a pin and glue, stick on eye whites and black pupils on top of them or satin stitch the eyes.

7 Sew white thread whiskers, as on the cat.

## *Purse*

You can make this purse to go in a handbag, or sew a cord on it and wear it as a shoulder purse. The instructions given are for sew-in interfacing.

**You will need**

30 cm × 30 cm of denim
40 cm × 40 cm of check gingham
30 cm × 15 cm of interfacing (medium iron-on or sew-in)
1 metre of narrow cord for shoulder purse
a Gingersnap press fastener and pliers, or a medium-size press fastener
thread

**Pattern**

Trace the pattern from the page and cut out.

**To cut out**

Cut out one front and one back in the denim, gingham and interfacing. Cut out two bias strips each 40 cm long × 3 cm wide in gingham (see page 35 for making bias strips).

**To make**

If using iron-on interfacing, press it on the gingham first.
1 Front: place the denim and gingham front shapes together with right sides facing and the interfacing on top. Match the edges and pin and tack together along the top straight edge only. Machine with straight stitches along this edge, with a 1-cm seam. Remove the tacking and turn the purse front right side out, with the interfacing sandwiched between the denim and gingham. Tack together all round. Machine top stitch close to the

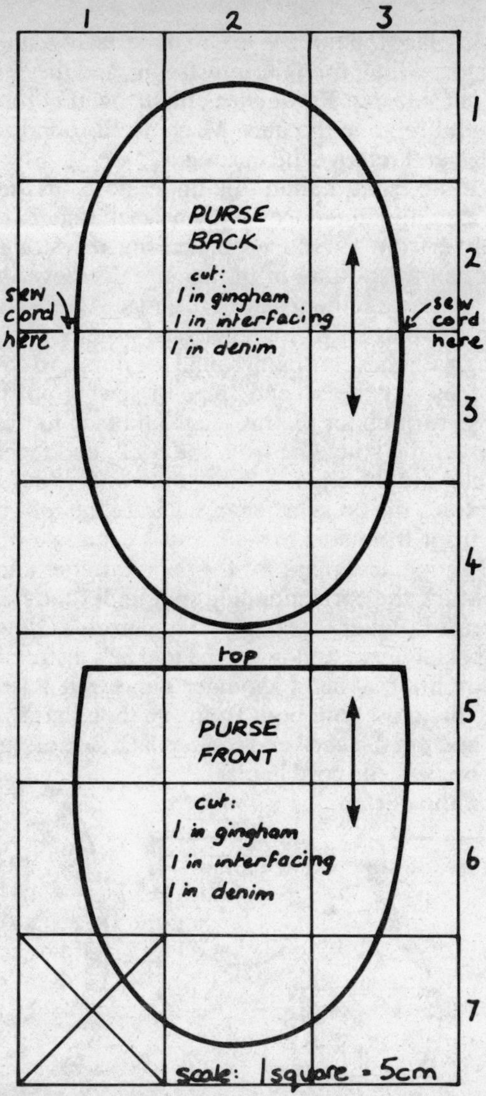
1
2
3
1
2
3
4
5
6
7
PURSE
BACK
cut:
1 in gingham
1 in interfacing
1 in denim
sew
cord
here
sew
cord
here
top
PURSE
FRONT
cut:
1 in gingham
1 in interfacing
1 in denim
scale: 1 square = 5cm

edge all round. When you have done this, remove the tacking.

2 Back: place the three layers of material together, with the gingham first, then the interfacing, and the denim on top, right side out. Pin and tack them together round the edges and remove the pins. Machine all round close to the edge and remove the tacking.

3 Place the front, denim side uppermost, on the purse back, matching the edges. Pin and tack together round the purse front curved edge, leaving the straight top edge open for putting in the money. Remove the pins and machine together close to the edge.

4 Join the bias strips together (see page 36). Sew bias binding with these strips all round the purse, to cover the raw edges. At the second stage of sewing on the bias binding, turn under the raw edge and tack to the purse front over the stitchline from the back, and machine in place close to the edge.

5 To attach the press fastener, measure the centre of the purse front from side to side, and 4 cm down from the straight edge, and mark for the press fastener underside here. Mark the corresponding spot under the flap. Sew on a press fastener (see page 42) or clip on a Gingersnap with special pliers, following the maker's instructions.

6 If you are making a shoulder purse, cut a length of cord to fit across your body from one shoulder, front and back, and pin the cord ends under each side of the purse flap. Oversew the cord in place.

7 Press the purse.

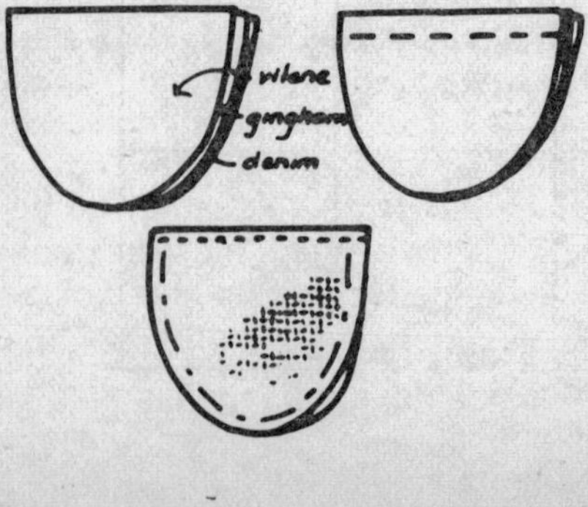


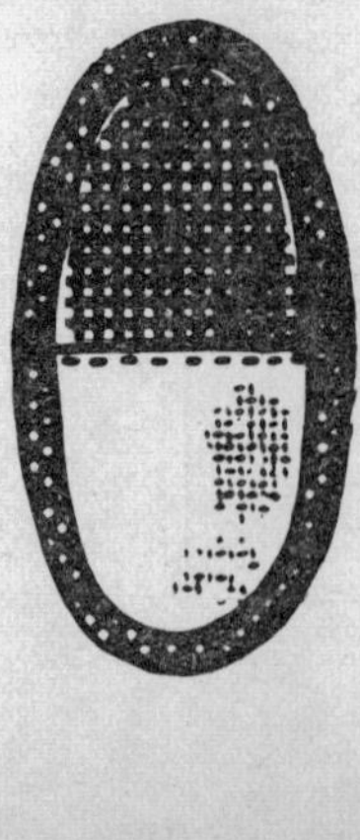

## *Duffel bag*

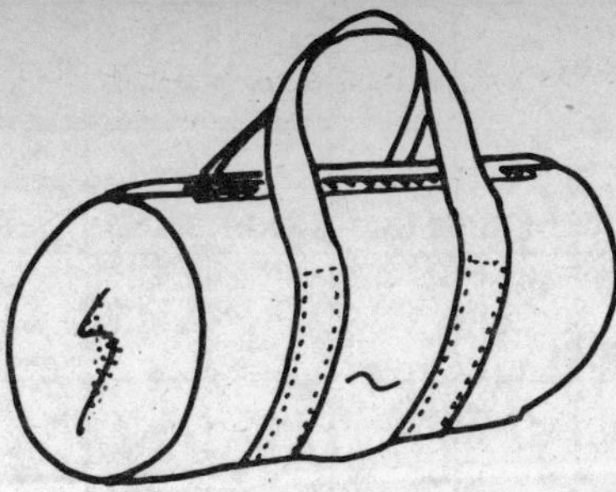

Bags like this are made out of every kind of material: corduroy, brocade, cotton. This one is made of strong nylon taffeta with twill braid handles. It is stitched with strong synthetic thread. When sewing tough material like this, be sure to have a sharp new needle on the sewing machine. Use straight stitch for this bag.

**You will need**

80 cm of 90-cm wide nylon taffeta
2 metres of twill braid 4 cm wide
1 metal zipper 40 cm long
synthetic thread

**Pattern**

Enlarge the pattern shapes from the chart and cut out.

**To cut out**

Cut out two sides and two ends. Transfer the marks from the pattern on to the material.

**To make**

1 Sew in the zipper. Place the duffel bag sides together right sides facing and tack together along one edge with a 2-cm seam allowance. Machine 3 cm from one end to join the seam for a short distance then change over to the zipper foot on the machine. (Refer to page 45 for detailed information on sewing in a zipper.) Sew the zipper to the tacked bag seam, above the machined end of the seam. The illustrations on page 132 show the steps described in the following text.

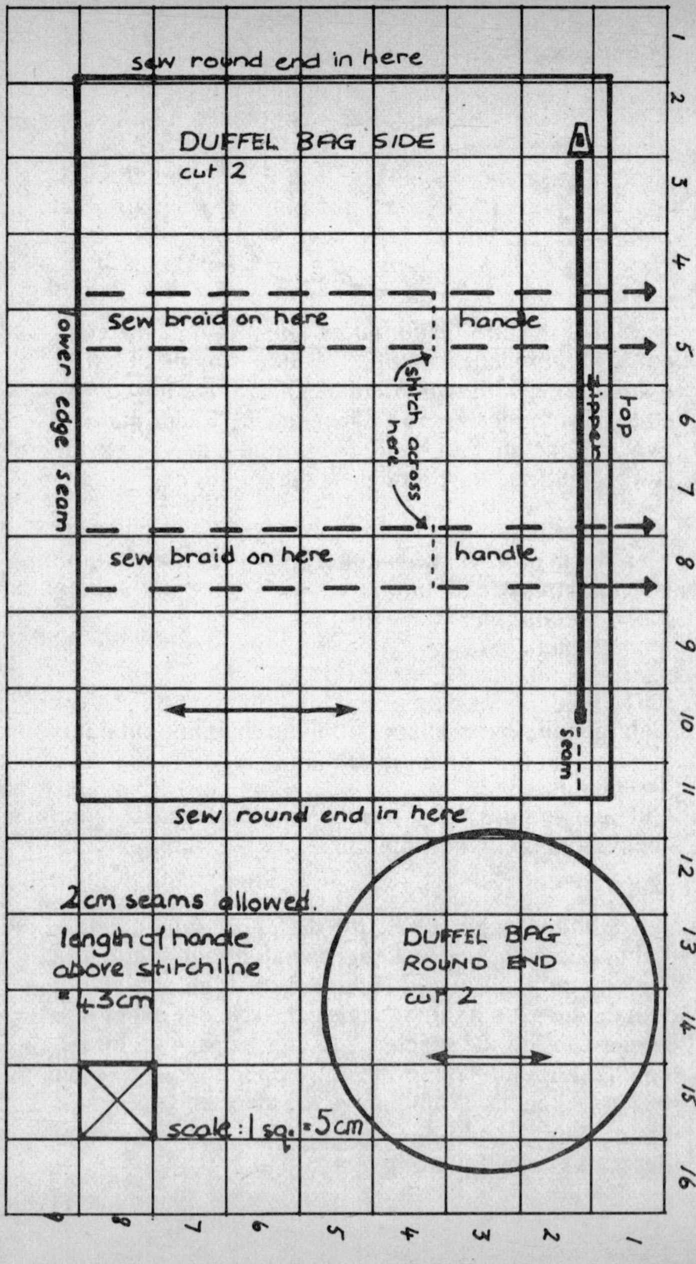
sew round end in here
DUFFEL BAG SIDE
cut 2
sew braid on here
handle
stitch across here
sew braid on here
handle
lower edge seam
zipper
top
seam
sew round end in here
2cm seams allowed.
length of handle above stitchline = 43cm
scale: 1 sq. = 5cm
DUFFEL BAG ROUND END
cut 2

2 With the zipper sewn in, remove the tacking. Turn the bag right side up and attach the braid for the handles in the following way. Cut the braid into two lengths, each a metre long. Starting from A at the raw edge, pin the braid along the placement line transferred from the pattern to point B, 8 cm from the zipper seam. Start again with the other end of the braid from point C at the raw edge further along, and pin this braid to the bag side as far as point D, again 8 cm from the zipper seam. Be careful not to twist the braid as you do this.

3 Turn the bag round and pin the second length of braid to the other side of the bag in the same way. You will now have two handles; overlap them across the zipper seam for the moment.

4 If you haven't already done so, change back to the general presser foot on the sewing machine. Tack the braid where pinned, remove the pins and machine it to the bag. For each of the four braid lengths, start at the raw edge, machine up one side of the braid close to the edge, stop at point B (or D as the case may be), pivot on the needle, machine across the braid, stop, turn, and machine down the other side to the end.

5 Pin the handles to the zipper seam, so they won't get mixed up in the other seam to be made now. Fold the bag back, right sides facing, and match the lower raw edges. Pin and tack along this edge for a 2-cm wide seam, then remove the pins and machine. Remove the tacking, unpin the handles and keep the bag wrong side out.

6 Open out one end of the bag, to form a tube shape, and take one circular end shape. Pin this shape to the bag, right sides facing, for a 2-cm seam. Work your way round until the entire circle has been pinned in place. Tack where pinned, and remove the pins. Machine, and remove the tacking.

7 Turn the bag right side out and open the zipper. Turn the bag wrong side out again with the zipper still open, and sew the other circle into the other end of the bag, right sides facing, as you did the first.

8 Turn the bag right side out and close the zipper.

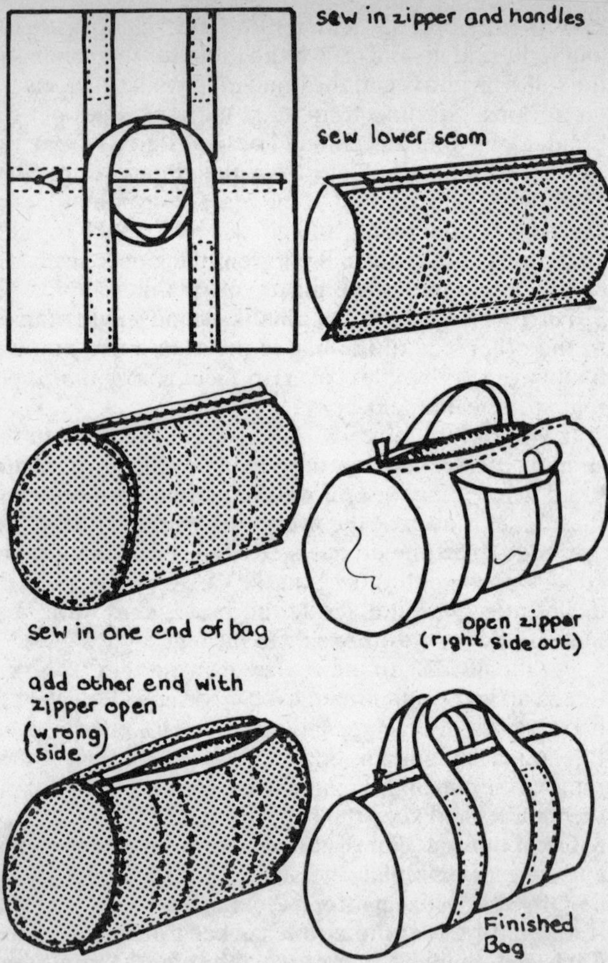


Note: if you have used material for your bag with the design going one way, up and down, be sure to have it the right way up for the circular bag ends, when you are sewing these in. Also, if your bag is made of plaid fabric, make sure the vertical and horizontal bands are the right way at each end.

## *Baby doll*

You could use an old baby stretch suit to make this doll, since that's what he's wearing. Or a T-shirt would do. Once you've made the stretch suit and hands, stuffed them, and added the head, the doll is made. He's called Moppet.

**You will need**

- 25 cm × 30 cm stretch terry towelling or T-shirt material: one each for the back and front
- 30 cm × 30 cm calico for the head and hands
- scraps of blue, red, pink and black felt for the features
- skein of wool for the hair
- thread for the stretch suit
- white thread for the calico
- pink and black thread for the features
- kapok
- knitting needle to push in the stuffing

**Pattern**

Trace the pattern shapes overleaf and cut out.

**To cut out**

Fold the towelling and pin the pattern 'fold edge' against the fold. Cut out. Repeat for the second shape. Cut out two head and four hand shapes in calico; and in felt: a red mouth, two pink cheeks, two blue eyes, two black pupils.

**To make**

1 Place the front and back shapes together, matching

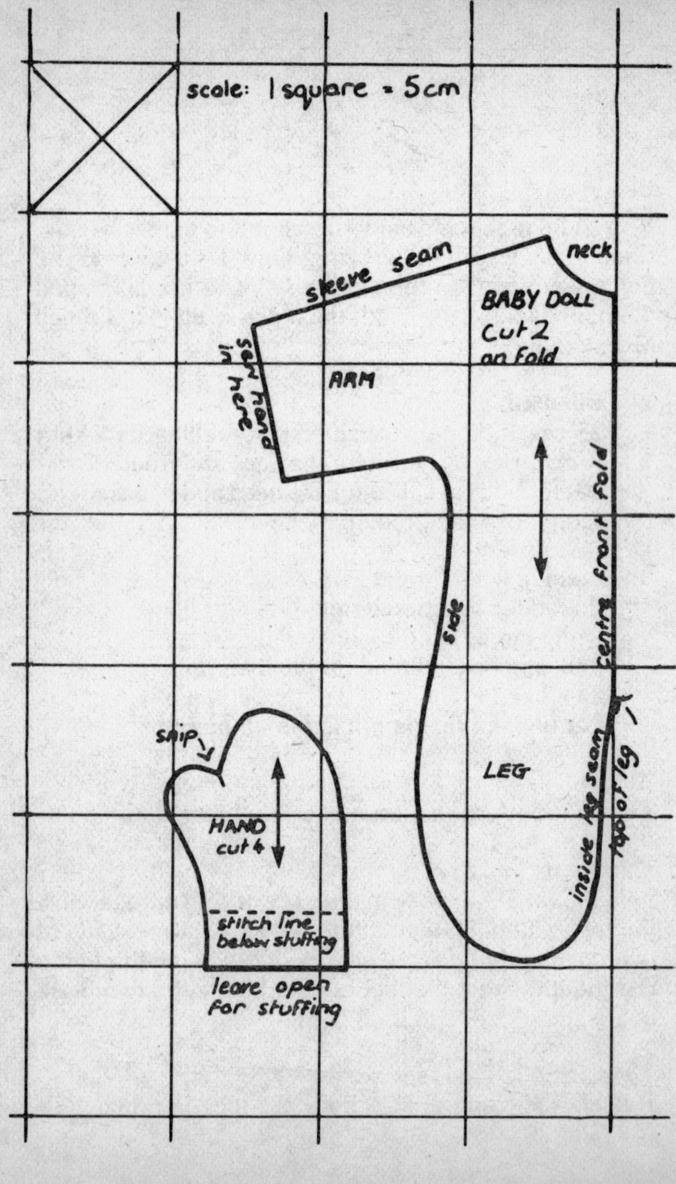

scale: 1 square = 5cm
sleeve seam
neck
BABY DOLL
Cut 2
on fold
sew hand in here
ARM
centre front fold
side
LEG
inside leg seam
top of leg
snip
HAND
cut 4
stitch line below stuffing
leave open for stuffing

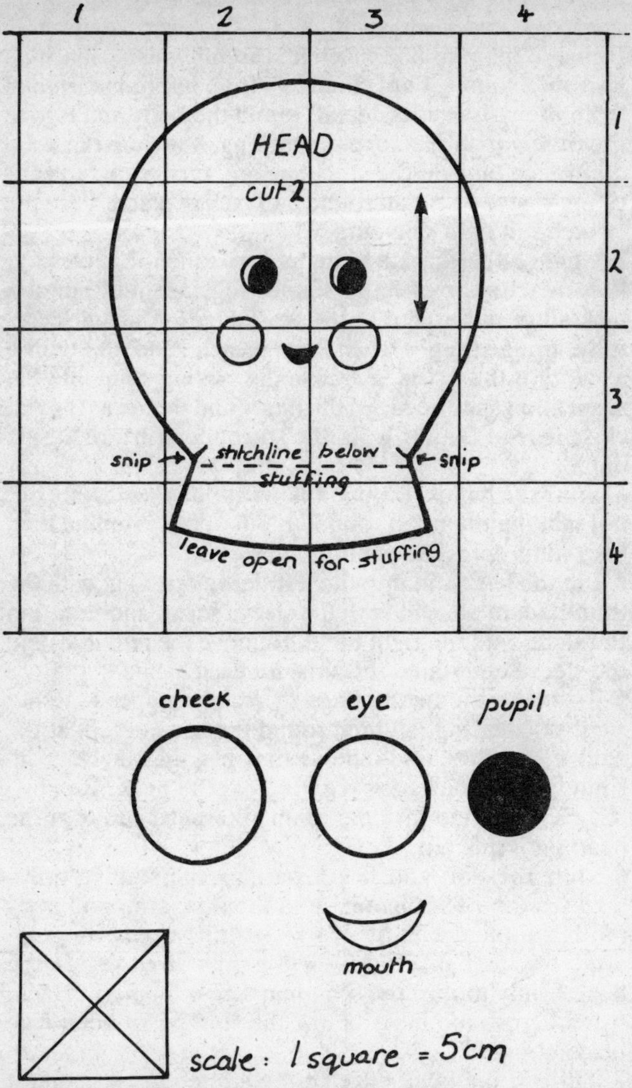
1
2
3
4
HEAD
cut 2
snip
stitchline below
snip
stuffing
leave open for stuffing
cheek
eye
pupil
mouth
scale: 1 square = 5cm

the edges, right sides facing, and the stripes at the seams if any. Pin all round except at the wrist and neck openings and tack, with a 1.5-cm seam allowance. Remove the pins and machine carefully, using machine knit stitch, along both shoulders from neck to wrist, and from the wrist underside all round the body and legs to the other wrist. Remove the tacking. Snip into the seam allowance outside the stitchline and turn back the ends of the sleeves 1 cm all round and tack in place. Turn the stretch suit right side out.

2 Change the thread to match the calico if necessary. Place each pair of hand shapes together and pin and tack all round except at the wrist edges. Machine carefully, using straight stitch, round each hand and thumb except for the wrists. Remove the tacking. Snip into the seam allowance between the finger and thumb as shown, close to, but not through, the stitchline. Turn right side out.

3 Stuff the hands through the wrist opening, firmly but not making them too rounded. Fill to the seamline then backstitch across above the stuffing.

4 Pin the left hand into the left sleeve opening, with the thumb seam aligned with the sleeve seam, and tack. Do the same with the right hand. Remove the pins and hem the sleeve end round the wrist for each hand.

5 To make the head, place the calico shapes together right sides facing, and pin round the head except at the neck edge. Tack and remove the pins, then machine all round where tacked, except across the neck. Remove the tacking, snip into the seam allowance and turn the head right side out.

6 Stuff the doll and head, pushing the stuffing down through the neck opening into the legs, arms and body (with the blunt end of a large knitting needle to help) until the doll is firmly filled to the neck. Stuff the head firmly too, to the seamline across the neck. Backstitch across the head below the stuffing to keep it in place.

7 Turn in the neck edge of the stretch suit and pin it

round the neck front and back. Tack and remove the pins. Hem the stretch suit neck edge all round to the neck twice, for extra strength.

8 Sew on the features. Hem the mouth in place; sew on the pink cheeks with a star of stitches, in red or pink thread; sew on the blue eyes and the pupils on top of them with black thread with a star of straight stitches.

9 Double a length of wool, and place it against the back of the doll's head. Make a stitch across the top of the loop to the head. Make another loop next to the first, take the needle under the material and sew that loop in place too. Continue for a row of loops round the head, to the sides of the face. Make more rows above until the head is covered, except for the face. Cut through the lower end of the loops to free the strands. If they are too long or uneven in length you can give the baby doll a haircut.

## *Tartan skirt*

When sewing tartan, the striped bands should be carefully matched wherever possible at the seams and overlaps. This skirt is made to fit a twelve-year-old, with a 65-cm waist, and finished length of 58 cm. As the material recommended for it is 140 cm wide, it shouldn't be difficult to alter the waist to your size, by letting out the gathers if you are larger, or drawing them in if you are smaller and adjusting the waistband size. So your main concern will be the length when buying the material for your skirt.

**You will need**

75 cm of 140-cm wide tartan material
3.5 cm × 82 cm firm sew-in interfacing (make up a strip this size)
2 buttons each 1 cm diameter
thread
1 kilt pin

**Pattern**
Enlarge the pattern from the charts overleaf and cut out. Cut out the waistband interfacing pattern separately.

**To cut out**
Cut out one skirt, one waistband in tartan material and one waistband interfacing. Transfer the pattern construction marks to the wrong side of the material.

**To make**
1 Adjust the sewing machine to straight stitch. The skirt overlap will go across from right to left. Mark the side of

the overlap, that is, the side with the darts, and run a row of machine stitching down the side 2 cm from the selvage. Cut away the selvage about 0.75 cm. To make the self-fringe use a needle to pick out the woven lengthwise threads beside this trimmed edge to make a narrow fringe, about 1 cm wide.
2 Along the underlap side edge, turn in a 1.5-cm hem and machine. A single hem is best with a woven selvage.

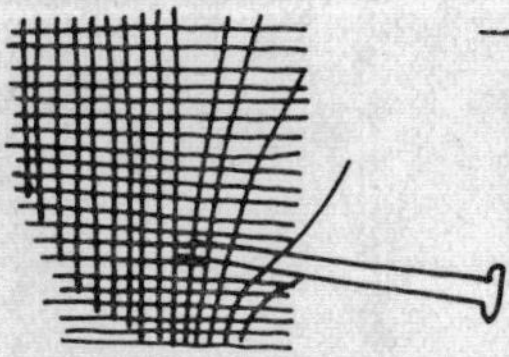
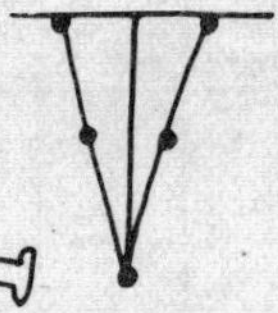
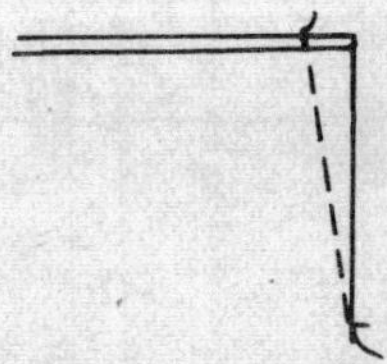

3 Darts are tapered pleats made in material to shape a garment to fit. They have been included here to fit your skirt at the waist – and to give you some practice at making them. Where the dart shape has been transferred from your pattern to the wrong side of your skirt, match the sides together and pin through the marks to join them. Tack from the top to the lowest point of the dart and remove the pins. Repeat for the second dart. Fold back the skirt so the dart protrudes at the right. Place the top end of the dart stitchline under the machine needle and machine down the dart, tapering it into the fold at the lowest point. Repeat for the second dart. Try to make them end exactly on the end of the pattern mark, so they are of equal length. Press.
4 Gather the skirt back by running a row of gathering stitches along the top of the skirt about 1.5 cm from the edge, where marked from your pattern. Anchor the thread end round a pin, but do not gather yet. (See page 103 for information about gathering.)
5 Make the waistband. Pin the interfacing to the waistband wrong side and tack round the edge. Remove the pins and machine round the interfacing close to the edge, using thread to match the tartan. The top edge of the interfacing should fit in the waistband centre fold.

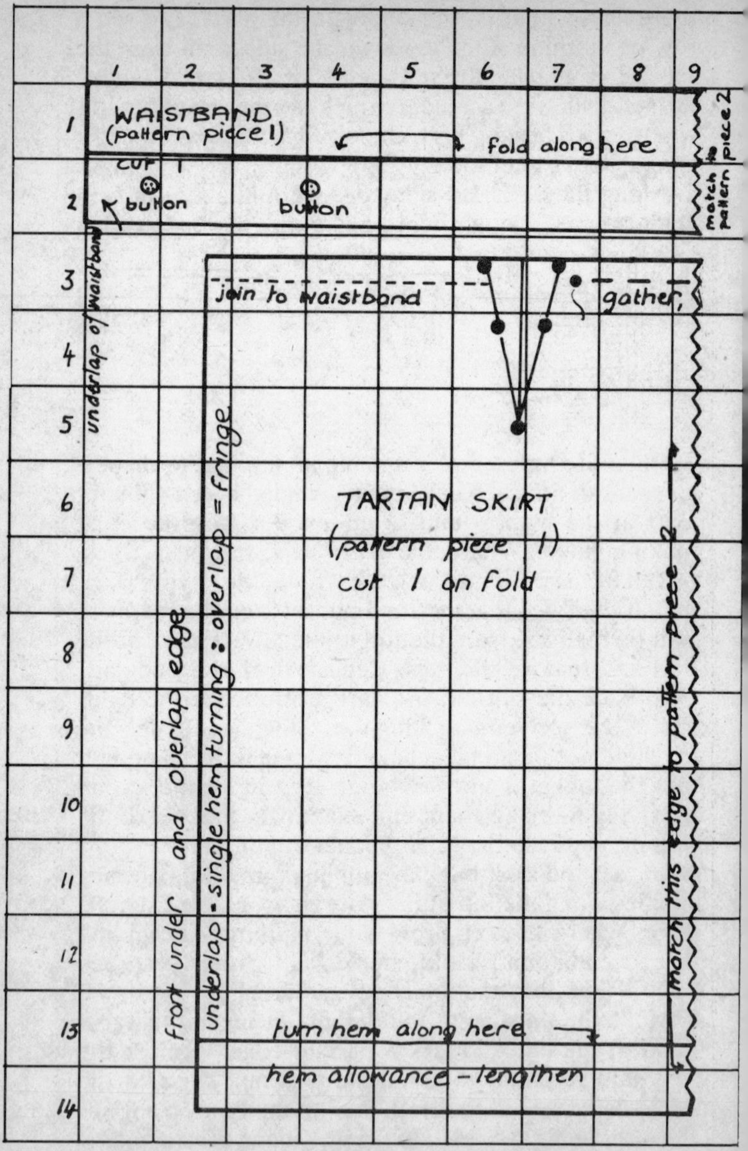

1 2 3 4 5 6 7 8 9
1 2 3 4 5 6 7 8 9 10 11 12 13 14
WAISTBAND
(pattern piece 1)
cut 1
fold along here
button
button
underlap of waistband
match to pattern piece 2
join to waistband
gather,
TARTAN SKIRT
(pattern piece 1)
cut 1 on fold
front under and overlap edge
underlap - single hem turning : overlap = fringe
match this edge to pattern piece 2
turn hem along here
hem allowance - lengthen

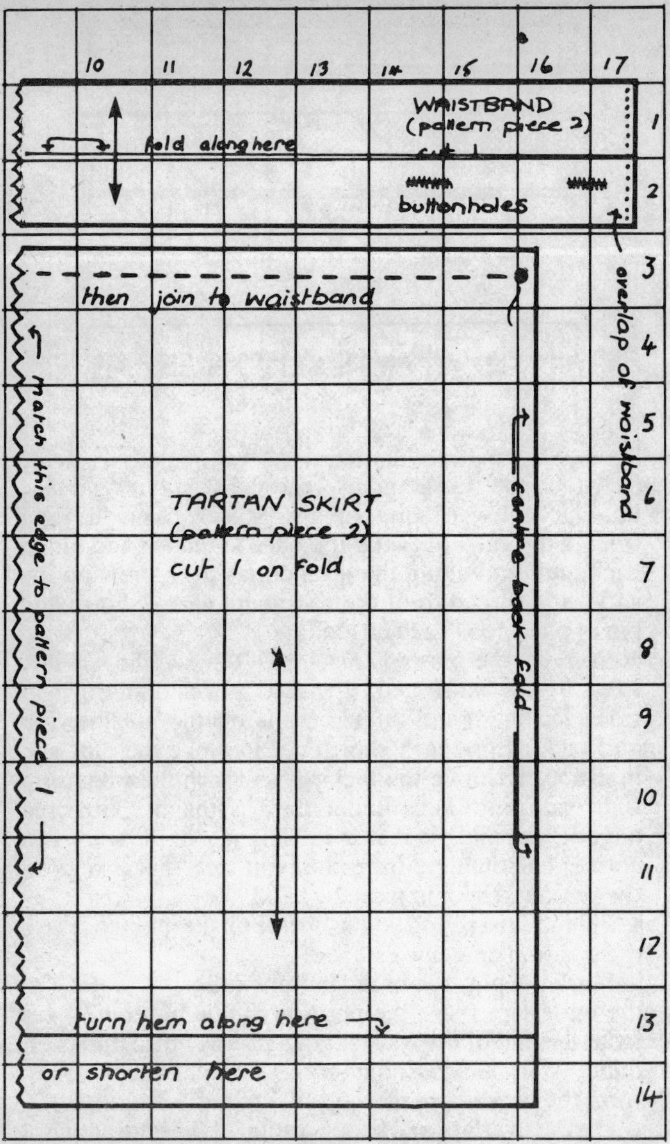

10
11
12
13
14
15
16
17
WAISTBAND
(pattern piece 2)
cut 1
fold along here
buttonholes
overlap of waistband
then join to waistband
match this edge to pattern piece 1
TARTAN SKIRT
(pattern piece 2)
cut 1 on fold
centre back fold
turn hem along here
or shorten here
1
2
3
4
5
6
7
8
9
10
11
12
13
14

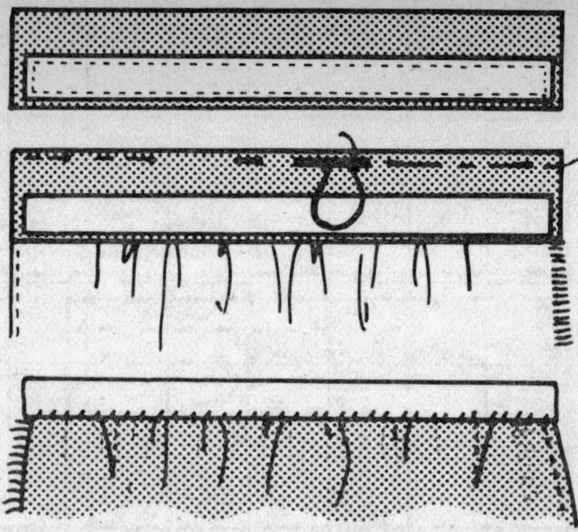

6 Attach the waistband. Spread the skirt out right side up. Place the waistband with its right side facing the right side of the skirt over the top edge as shown and pin at each end, and along the level darts edge. Draw up the gathering thread to fit the waistband where shown and pin in place too. Tack all along.
7 Remove the pins and machine. Remove the tacking. Press up the waistband, then fold it back on itself right sides facing so the interfacing is on the outside. Pin and tack across each short end. Remove the pins and machine. Remove the tacking, and turn the waistband right side out. Turn under the waistband unattached edge 1.5 cm and pin it to the wrong side of the skirt, just above the stitchline from the right side. Tack, remove the pins, and hem in place by hand.
8 Pin the skirt round you to decide on the overlap. Mark the position on the waistband.
9 Mark the position of the buttons and buttonholes. On the underlap, mark the position of one buttton 2.5 cm from the end of the waistband, half-way down the waistband. Mark the position of the second button 1.5 cm from the overlap mark.

On the overlap, mark the position of the buttonhole at

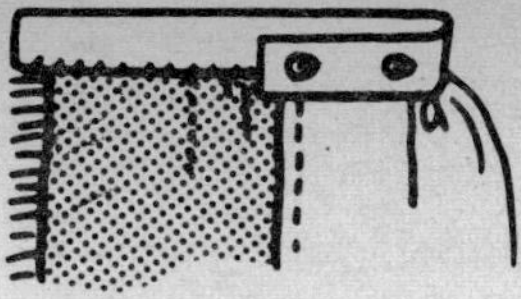

the end of the waistband, so it starts 1.5 cm from the waistband end half-way down the waistband. Mark the other buttonhole to begin from the centre of the second button. Sew on the two buttons, and embroider buttonholes to correspond, using buttonhole stitch (see page 41). You could sew machined buttonholes instead if your machine will do this.

10 For the hem, trim the edge of the skirt level along one of the tartan bands. Pin skirt tape along it on the right side to cover the raw edge, so the raw edge comes about half-way across on the wrong side of the tape. Tack all along and remove the pins. Machine close to the tape edge.

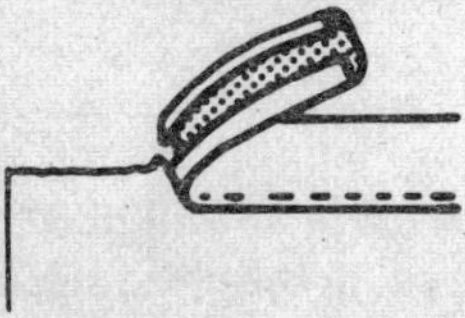
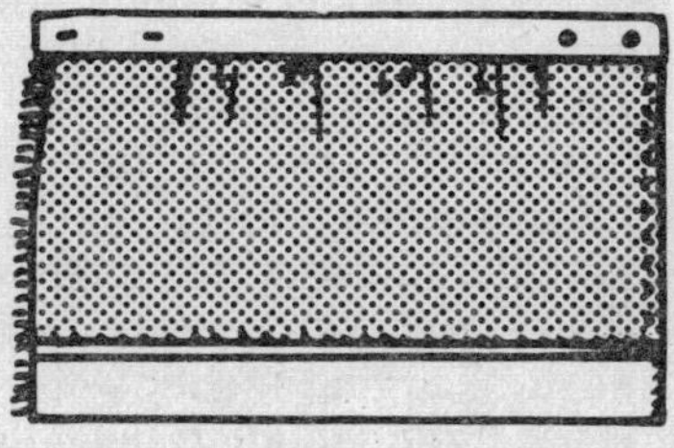

11 Turn up the hem. Turn the skirt right side out, and measure the length you have decided from the waistband. Mark with chalk or horizontal pins at the length, once again following the convenient line of the nearest tartan band to make sure you are keeping level. If you are sewing plain material, check the hem depth (the space between the length marks and the skirt edge) with a measuring gauge or ruler, for an equal depth all along.

Fold the hem up along this marked edge and pin along. Tack and remove the pins everywhere. Try on the skirt to check that the length is satisfactory, and press the hem. Slipstitch the hem to the skirt along the tape edge as described on page 25.

12 Press the skirt and overlap, and fasten with a kilt pin.

# Bought Pattern Project

A pattern has everything you need to enable you to make the garment, toy, or other item pictured on the packet: the paper shapes to pin to the material and cut out; the complete illustrated sewing instructions; and on the outside of the packet, the amounts of material, buttons, elastic, etc., you will need to buy for your size. If you read the pattern instructions carefully and carry them out at every stage, you'll be sure of success.

Patterns are usually available in the dressmaking materials department in a store, or you can order them by post. The main pattern manufacturers sell magazines with the latest designs for you to choose from.

This pattern has been chosen because it is a simple, classic style and shows many of the features that are likely to crop up in dressmaking. You may not be able to obtain this exact design as time goes by, but you are sure to be able to find one very similar.

**Your pattern size**

If you intend to make something to wear, you will need to know your pattern size. This is based on the chest size for a dress or coat and the waist size for skirts or trousers. For babies and toddlers height and weight apply, too.

**Pattern categories**

Pattern sizes are scaled for different groups of people: Children; Misses; Boys and Teen-boys. Girls' patterns are designed for sizes 7 to 14, roughly comparable with the average size for that age, and called *Girls*, and for *Young Junior/Teen*, designed, as they say, for pre-teen and teen figures. So buy a pattern for the group that is suitable for your age and size.

**Which materials to buy for the pattern?**

Once you have bought your pattern, you are going to need the materials to make it, including thread, zipper, buttons: whatever the design requires. To find out how

# Style 3099

much to buy, turn the pattern packet over and look at the back. There is a lot of important information printed on it.

First there is the maker's name and the serial number of the pattern and a description of the garments you can make from the patterns in it. This is worth reading because you will learn from it what sort of pockets you will be making, or whether the garment is lined or unlined, and other details. Also it will mention somewhere whether the pattern is suitable for knitted material or not. Probably there will be a picture of the back views, or perhaps the shapes of the pattern pieces. And most important, there will be a chart to tell you how much material to buy.

The pattern shown on page 145 includes several different garments, some of them using the same pattern pieces. You might decide to make *View 1*: a shirt dress with long sleeves, say in size 12. To find out how much material this requires, ring size 12 and *View 1*, and the width of the fabric you have chosen, 90 cm wide, in the section headed *View 1*. Look along the line beside the ringed material width under the size, and the amount of material is there: 2.7 metres. For 115-cm wide fabric the amount needed would have been 2.10 metres; for 140-cm wide, 1.7 metres, and for 165-cm wide, 1.5 metres. The chart shows that the dress doesn't need lining, but 40 cm of interfacing is needed to stiffen the collar.

**Notions**

This is the list of sewing items other than material needed to make the garment on this Style pattern headed: *To complete garment*. For the shirt dress, *View 1*, only three buttons, thread and a belt are needed, though you could make the latter.

It is a good idea to buy everything needed at the same time, put them in a clean plastic bag and pin the bag to the material. Before you leave the shop, check the pattern packet in case there's anything you've missed. It is annoying to get home with something important missing.

Select **PATTERN PIECES** for the garment you are making.

**14 pieces given**

| | |
|---|---|
| view 1 | A B C D E F |
| view 2–3 | A C D E F |
| view 4 | G H K L |
| view 5 and trousers | B G H K L M N P R |
| trousers | M N P R |

## dress · tunic or blouse
## pinafore or top and trousers

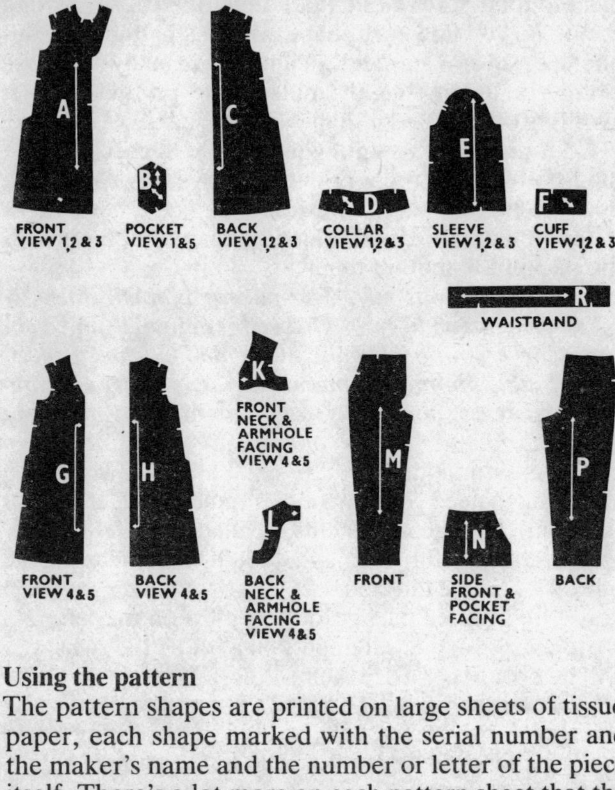


### Using the pattern

The pattern shapes are printed on large sheets of tissue paper, each shape marked with the serial number and the maker's name and the number or letter of the piece itself. There's a lot more on each pattern sheet that the instructions explain. These consist of one, two, or even three printed and illustrated sheets of paper, which tell you everything you need to know about making up the garments pictured on the envelope.

## *View 1: a shirt dress*

I am going to explain step by step how to use the pattern to make the shirt dress.

The pattern has a list of the pieces needed for the dress and a drawing of their shapes, with the code number or letter printed on them. The first job is to underline these pieces, then spread out the sheets of patterns to find them. As you find each shape, and in a pattern like this one with several garments in it there are many to choose from, cut it out roughly, outside the printed outline, avoiding other pattern shapes close by, and set it aside.

Continue like this until you are able to check against the list on the instructions that you have found them all, down to the last small cuff or facing. The other pattern sheets and pieces can be folded up again and returned to the packet for another time.

The instructions say: *The pattern is made to body measurements with 'ease' allowed for design, fit and comfort. Check your back waist, sleeve and finished lengths. If in doubt, pin pattern pieces together and try on carefully. Make any alterations to the pattern before pinning it to the fabric.*

Let us assume that you are size 12. This is where you are going to need your own measurements list. If you put the pattern measurements, called *standard body measurements*, for your size (you'll find them on the packet), and the finished back length of the dress (which you'll find on the packet too), in a list on the left, and write your own measurements on a list on the right, you will be able to compare them.

You can see where the pattern is going to need some changes. Small changes can be made at the fitting stage, but big changes have to be made to the pattern before you start.

| *Size 12* | *Mary – aged 12* |
|---|---|
| Standard body measurements | Her measurements |
| Breast: 76 cm | 74 cm |
| Waist: 65 cm | 63 cm |
| Hip: 81 cm | 80 cm |
| Back: neck to waist: 34.5 cm | 33 cm |
| Finished back length: 86 cm | 84 cm |
| Sleeve length – taken from sleeve and cuff pattern: 58 cm | 55 cm |

**To lengthen a pattern**

Have a piece of squared dressmaking paper, or other paper, on the table. Cut the pattern shape you want to lengthen along the printed shortening or lengthening lines, spread the pattern apart over the paper, to the amount you want to add to the length, and pin the pattern to the paper, keeping the edges parallel. Redraw the outlines so they are even and cut out along the outside. Make wider in the same way. See diagram overleaf.

**To shorten a pattern**

Make an even pleat along the shortening or lengthening lines to take out the amount by which you want to shorten the garment, fold back the pattern edge for an even outline, and pin both the pleat and outline. Make narrower in the same way.

**Ease**

'Ease' is the extra room allowed in a pattern for a comfortable fit. Imagine skin-tight garments – they wouldn't give any room for bending or stretching. So they have to be allowed 'ease'. 'Ease' is used in another way in dressmaking, to describe fitting a slightly longer edge to a slightly shorter edge, as when setting in sleeves.

**Know your pattern markings**

Look again at one of the printed pattern shapes you have cut out; you will see there are various symbols and lines which are sometimes repeated. These are a guide to using the pattern.

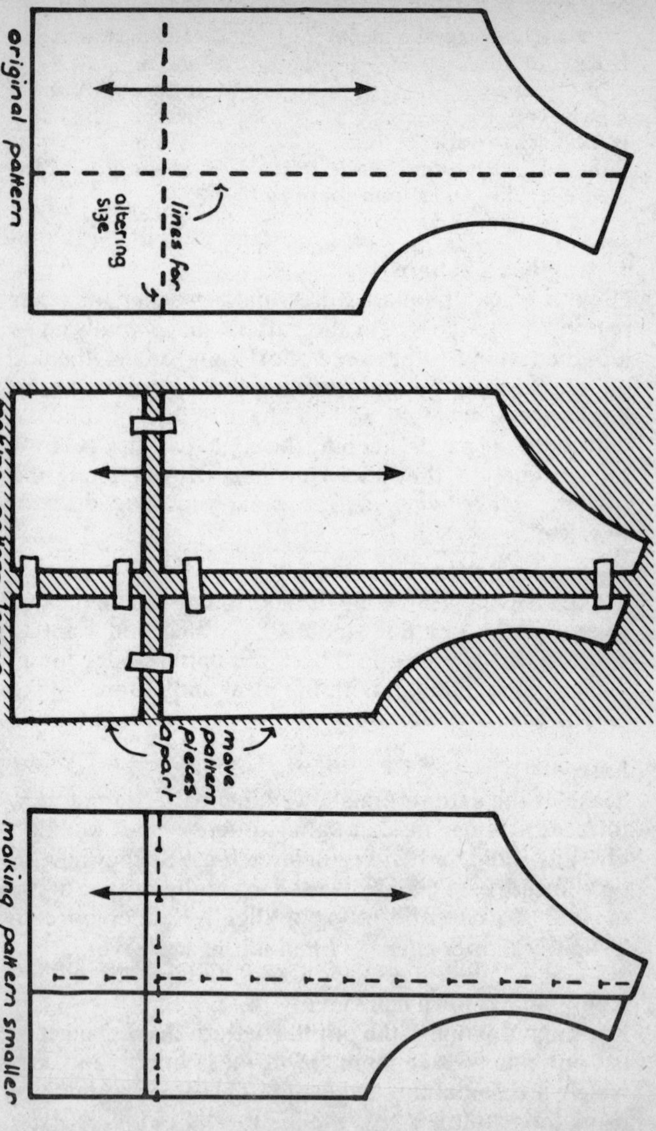
original pattern
lines for altering size
making pattern larger
move pattern pieces apart
making pattern smaller

## KNOW YOUR PATTERN MARKINGS

**Straight grain:** Place an even distance from selvage or a straight thread.

**Fold grain:** Place on fold of fabric.

**Cutting line**

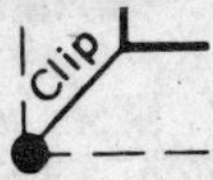


**Clip:** Short line indicates where to release the seam allowance by clipping.

**Construction symbols.**

**Notches:** Blocked in for easier cutting.

**Dots**

**Triangles**

**Lengthening and shortening lines**

**Stitching lines:** For darts, seams, etc.

**Directional arrows:** Stitch seams in direction indicated.

**Solid lines:** Indicate centers, fold lines, placement for pockets or trimmings.

**Buttonholes**

1 Straight grain of fabric: (symbol: double arrow). When pinning on the pattern, this must be placed parallel to the selvage.
2 Fold: (symbol: bent double arrow). This must be placed against folded material.
3 Cutting line: (symbol: a solid line with scissors). Cut out along this line.
4 Lengthen or shorten here: (symbol: a solid cutting line with these words) means what it says.
5 Stitching lines: (symbol: long broken lines with machine presser foot) means stitch along here.
6 Other solid lines: fold lines, such as the centre fold line of a waistline, or pocket placement, have the explanation

printed beside them on the pattern piece.

7 Button and buttonhole placement: (symbols: a button; a buttonhole-shape line) means sew a button, or a buttonhole, here.

8 Clip: (symbol: a line into the seam allowance). Cut a snip into the seam allowance, but not through the stitchline.

9 Construction symbols: (black diamonds, spots, squares, triangles). Diamonds are seam-matching points, and indicate where you should match edges together when joining parts of a garment. Single notches match single, double notches match double. Spots are matching points across a piece of material, such as the sides of darts. The same goes for other shapes.

10 Zipper placement: (symbol: a zipper on a seamline). Sew the zipper in here.

11 Gather here: (symbol: on the gather edge: a broken line with a black spot at each end; on the line the gather is to be joined to, an ordinary stitching line with a spot at each end). Gather the gathering edge to fit the opposite edge, matching the black marker spots.

Before pinning the pattern to the material for cutting out, the material itself will need to be checked over. You will want to be sure it won't shrink after you have gone to all the trouble of sewing it.

Many materials do not shrink, such as synthetic fabrics, or some may have been pre-shrunk at the mill. If not, you can pre-shrink material yourself. (Denim can sometimes be a problem here.) See pages 16 to 18 for more information on this, and about straightening the selvages and ends of the material.

**Laying out and cutting out your pattern**

Even with a simple pattern there will be what appears to be an endless number of little black and white charts called cutting layouts. These are the charts which show you how to place the pattern pieces on your material. You only need to be concerned with the ones for the garment you are making (for our example: *View 1* dress) and for

## CUTTING LAYOUTS

KEY: Fabric | Pattern printed side up | Pattern printed side down

FOR DOUBLE THICKNESS: Fold fabric with RIGHT side INSIDE.
FOR SINGLE THICKNESS: Place fabric RIGHT side UP.
When pattern pieces extend beyond fold of fabric, cut out all pieces except pieces that extend. Then open out fabric onto the right side and cut extending pieces on single thickness.

**SCISSORS INDICATE EXACT CUTTING LINES**

***NOTE: On smaller sizes pieces interlock more closely.**

**VIEW 1** dress

**90 cm fabric without nap** *
**all sizes**

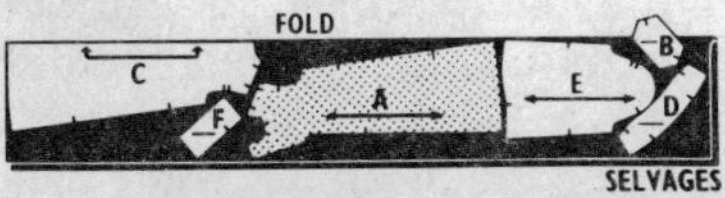


**140 cm fabric with nap** *
**all sizes**

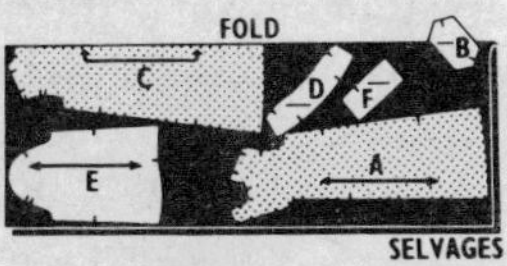


**150 cm fabric without nap** *
**sizes 7, 8, 10**

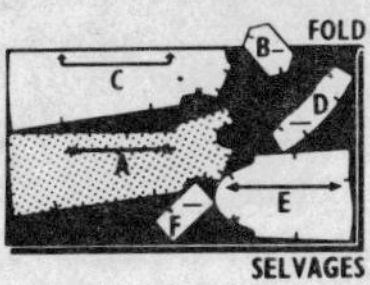


your width of material. There is one other difference: if your material is 'with nap', such as velvet, or corduroy, then you would need to choose a 'with nap' cutting layout for the dress and width material. (See above.)

Notice that for the 'without nap' cutting layout, the dress patterns are pinned on in opposite directions, in the 'with nap' cutting layout, they are side by side, to take account of the fact that velvet, for instance, must be cut one way.

**Other features of a cutting layout**
The material is represented by the solid black rectangle. Often along one side – not necessarily the top edge – you will see the word FOLD. This means that you should fold the material this way. The word SELVAGES appears too, where the selvages should be on your folded material to go with this layout.

Place the pattern pieces on the material following the cutting layout.

Once you have laid out your material, folded to correspond with the cutting layout, place the pattern pieces along it as shown on the chart, with the straight grain of fabric and fold symbols where they are on the layout. The shading of a pattern shape has a meaning: white means that the printed side of the pattern is uppermost, dots or diagonal lines mean that the printed side is laid against the material. Where you see one shape sticking out of the side of the layout, sometimes with a star on it, this means that after you have cut out the other pieces, you open the material out, and cut this shape through one layer only. Before beginning to cut out, make sure all the shapes are pinned on the fabric, so you know they will all fit.

**Pin on your pattern**
Keeping the pattern and material level together, pin the pattern in place round the edge in the seam allowance, using a pin about every 10 cm. When placing the next pattern shape in position, it doesn't matter if the rough edges overlap, so long as the printed shapes are kept separate.

**Cutting out**
Use cutting-out scissors, and start from the edge of the material close to the edge of the pattern cutting line. Cut through both layers of material at one time where

required, unless it is very thick, when you will need to cut through the top layer first, and then the under layer. When you come to a notch or a fine detail, cut round it to begin with. Later you can use small scissors to cut round the notches or small shapes exactly. Keep the pattern pinned to the material until you have transferred the pattern marks.

**Marking your fabric**

It will save you a lot of time and trouble if you transfer the construction marks on the pattern on to your material. This almost amounts to printing the pattern on the material so you know exactly where to sew on a pocket or button, or place a dart. Here are some methods you can use, which are quite fun to carry out.

*Tracing wheel and dressmaker's carbon paper*, used for smooth material. As explained on page 10, a tracing wheel is a metal or plastic wheel with a serrated edge, fitted into a small handle, and is used with dressmaker's carbon paper – coloured, non-smudgy carbon paper made especially for use with material. You will need a ruler too, and a piece of board to protect the table from the sharp wheel marks.

The material, with the pattern pinned on, preferably so that the carbon will be over the wrong side of the material, is placed on the board. Slip the carbon, coloured side against the material, between the pattern and the fabric, where you wish to transfer a mark, such as a dart. Place the ruler beside the straight line of the dart, and roll the wheel beside it, following the printed pattern shape. Where there's a marker spot, draw a little cross. When you remove the pattern there will be a little shape in dots on the material.

*Tailor's chalk*, used with ruler and pins, for plain materials where chalk shows up, but not carbon dots.

1 Stick pins through the pattern marking from the right side of the material, then turn the material over.

2 Rub tailor's chalk where the pin is showing through.
3 Remove the pins and pattern.
4 Join the chalk dots with a ruler to form a line.

*Tailor's tacking*, used for thick woollen or other material which will not show carbon dots or chalk marks.
1 Keep the pattern pinned to the material. Thread a needle with double thread. Bring it through the material and pattern mark, and put it back through on the same spot, leaving a loop of thread on top.
2 Take a stitch along under the material and repeat.
3 Unpin the pattern and pull off. Pull the layers of material gently apart and snip between the stitches. A row of thread tufts will mark the pattern shapes on the material.

**Making the garment**

When you begin to carry out the step-by-step instructions for making up the chosen garment it may seem as if you are working back to front. For example, often the first thing you sew on is the pocket, but it is much easier to do this job before the dress is made up, on a flat piece of material.

The pattern for the shirt dress has the instructions in sections called UNITS. First the pocket is sewn on, and then UNIT 1 is joining the shoulders. UNIT 2 is making the collar and sewing it on, and turning back the dress opening facings. UNIT 3 is sewing the main seams. UNIT 4 is making the sleeves and cuffs and sewing them in. UNIT 5 is sewing the hem, and UNIT 6 is sewing a button and button loop at the neck.

*Pockets* The pocket on the shirt dress is a patch pocket, made by folding over a double pocket shape. Before it is turned right side out, the corners are snipped away to reduce the bulk. When the pocket is turned right side out, the edges of the opening are turned in to neaten them and oversewn with slipstitch. After being pressed, the pocket is pinned to the dress front where the transferred pattern mark indicates its position, and tacked in place down the sides and round the lower edge. The pocket can be invisibly sewn in place by hand with slip-hemming or machined with topstitch (see page 57), using the inside of the presser foot to help you make a straight stitchline.

UNIT 1: stay-stitching the neck edge and joining the shoulder seams. Use straight stitching on the machine throughout.

*Stay-stitching* is a single line of straight machine stitching round an edge to prevent it from fraying or stretching out of shape. The tartan skirt on page 138 has a line of stay-stitching down the side to secure the fringe.

*Shoulder seams* are placed together right sides facing. The pattern instructions don't say 'right sides facing' but you can see from the way the seam is folded back that the dotted sides, which mean the right sides, are placed together.

The notches are matched to make sure that the seams are accurately joined. Here is an example of the other use of the term 'ease'. The back edges are very slightly longer than the front edges, so the front edges have to be stretched a little, and the back edges cramped a little to stitch them together without creasing. This is so the dress will fit the shoulder comfortably.

UNIT 2: making and sewing on the collar, and the shaped facings for the front opening.

The shirt dress collar is made with two layers of material with a layer of interfacing between. Like the pocket, the collar is trimmed at the corners, and the interfacing outside the stitchline, and with thick material, the seam itself, leaving about 75 mm of the seam allowance, before being turned right side out. You need some seam allowance to prevent the material fraying through the seam.

*Clip curves* When you read this term in the instructions, it means snip into a curved edge in the seam allowance, but not through the stitchline, so that when you turn the part right side out it will lie flat.

*Join the collar to the neck edge* There are a number of ways for joining the collar to the neck edge. This shirt dress collar is sewn on with a shaped facing.

UNIT 3: making and finishing the main seams of the dress.

With this pattern, the shoulder seams and collar are already complete. Now, right sides facing, the centre front and side seams are joined, matching the seam edges, and the notches. After the tacking has been removed, the edges of the seam allowances will need to be finished neatly. Press the seams open when finished from the wrong side, then from the right side.

UNIT 4: making the sleeves and buttoned cuffs; joining the cuffs to the sleeves, and sewing the sleeves into the armholes. The shirt dress has long sleeves, gathered at the top, and at the wrist into buttoned cuffs, similar to those on a regulation school blouse.

Above the cuff there is a short faced opening in the sleeve, and making this is the first job when you come to the sleeve. First of all the triangular shape outline for the opening will need to have been transferred from the pattern. After the facing has been stitched in place, the space between the stitchlines is cut out, as close as possible into the point without cutting through the machine stitches, but with a narrow seam allowance lower down. This facing is then turned to the wrong side of the sleeve, and secured to the sleeve with slipstitch.

*Sleeve seams* The sleeves are folded right sides facing, matching the sides and notches, and joined with plain seams.

*Cuffs* The cuff overlaps from the outside wrist at the faced sleeve opening. Cuffs are usually interfaced like the collar and waistband. When finishing off the cuffs, buttons are sewn on the underlaps, and buttonholes in the overlaps, where marked.

*Sewing the sleeve into the armhole* Check that you are sewing the left sleeve into the left armhole, and the right sleeve into the right armhole. The front of the sleeve usually has a single notch, and the back a double notch, and so does the armhole, so this can be your guide. Machine both sleeves into the armhole where tacked, and then all round a second time close to the first. A sleeve seam is pulled and tugged a lot in wear and needs to be extra strong.

UNIT 5: turning up and sewing the skirt hem. This can be done as described in the pattern or as explained on page 143.

UNIT 6: sewing a button on one side of the neck opening, and a thread loop at the opposite side. A thread loop is made in the following way. Thread a needle with double thread, and oversew to secure at the top right. Take the thread down a stitch along the edge, leaving it loose, for a loop to fit over the button. Secure this loop with one or two oversewing stitches at the lower end. Take the thread back up for a matching loop, and secure it to the edge, and repeat once more. Pull these threads forming loops of equal size. Rethread the needle, and starting at the top, sew buttonhole stitch along the loop and secure it at the end.

**Fitting**

Fitting the dress to your general measurements should have been taken care of when adjusting the pattern. But you may need to make some minor adjustments. When you are trying on the finished dress for hem length, wear it over underclothes and with shoes, with the openings overlapped and pinned or fastened, and the belt on.

1 At the early stages, it is a good idea to try on the dress to check the fit of the shoulders and the collar, and that it is an easy comfortable fit with seams that hang down vertically. It should not be too tight.

2 If you find you need to make an alteration, mark the change with tailor's chalk or pins, and tack it again. Don't cut away the material until you are sure you have got it right.

3 Try on the dress before you machine in the sleeve. It should sit neatly around the shoulder, and be comfortable with your arm bent or straight.

# More Beaver Books

We hope you have enjoyed this Beaver Book. Here are some of the other titles:

**250 More Things to Send Off For** A Beaver original. Posters, wall-charts, jigsaws, jewellery, models to make – details of all kinds of exciting things you can send for through the post, most of which are either free or at pocket-money prices. Written by Elizabeth Gundrey, author of *Send Off For It*, and illustrated by Susie Lacome

**The Beaver Holiday Quiz** A Beaver original. From Greek mythology to pop music and films, this book is packed with questions on all kinds of topics to keep the whole family guessing for hours. Written by Robin May and illustrated by Alan Rogers

**The Gooseberry** A story about the ups and downs of Ellie Ferguson, a young Edinburgh girl, which will delight all older readers. Written by Joan Lingard, author of the popular 'Maggie' books

These and many other Beavers are available from your local bookshop or newsagent, or can be ordered direct from: Hamlyn Paperback Cash Sales, PO Box 11, Falmouth, Cornwall TR10 9EN. Send a cheque or postal order made payable to the Hamlyn Publishing Group, for the price of the book plus postage at the following rates:
UK: 40p for the first book, 18p for the second book, and 13p for each additional book ordered to a maximum charge of £1.49;
BFPO and Eire: 40p for the first book, 18p for the second book, plus 13p per copy for the next 7 books and thereafter 7p per book;
OVERSEAS: 60p for the first book and 18p for each extra book.

New Beavers are published every month and if you would like the *Beaver Bulletin*, a newsletter which tells you about new books and gives a complete list of titles and prices, send a large stamped addressed envelope to:

**Beaver Bulletin**
The Hamlyn Group
Astronaut House
Feltham
Middlesex TW14 9AR

203239